GESTALT

FOR BEGINNERS

Writers and Readers Publishing, Inc.
P.O. Box 461, Village Station
New York, NY 10014

Writers and Readers Limited
35 Britannia Row
London N1 8QH
Tel: 0171 226 3377
Fax: 0171 359 1454
e-mail: begin@writersandreaders.com

A Writers and Readers Documentary Comic Book
Copyright © 1998
ISBN # 0-86316-258-4 Trade
1 2 3 4 5 6 7 8 9

Printed in Finland by WS Bookwell

Beginners Documentary Comic Books are published by Writers and Readers Publishing Inc. Its trademark, consisting of the words "For Beginners, Writers and Readers Documentary Comic Books" and the Writers and Readers logo, is registered in the U.S. Patent and Trademark Office and in other countries.

Writers and Readers—publishing FOR BEGINNERS books continuously since 1975:

1975: Cuba · 1976: Marx · 1977: Lenin · 1978: Nuclear Power · 1979: Einstein · Freud · 1980: Mao · Trotsky · 1981: Capitalism · 1982: Darwin · Economists · French Revolution · Marx's Kapital · Food · Ecology · 1983: DNA · Ireland · 1984: London · Peace · Medicine · Orwell · Reagan · Nicaragua · Black History · 1985: Marx Diary · 1986: Zen · Psychiatry · Reich · Socialism · Computers · Brecht · Elvis · 1988: Architecture · Sex · JFK · Virginia Woolf · 1990: Nietzsche · Plato · Malcolm X · Judaism · 1991: WW II · Erotica · African History · 1992: Philosophy · Rainforests · Malcolm X · Miles Davis · Islam · Pan Africanism · 1993: Psychiatry · Black Women · Arabs & Israel · Freud · 1994: Babies · Foucault · Heidegger · Hemingway · Classical Music · 1995: Jazz · Jewish Holocaust · Health Care · Domestic Violence · Sartre · United Nations · Black Holocaust · Black Panthers · Martial Arts · History of Clowns · 1996: Opera · Biology · Saussure · UNICEF · Kierkegaard · Addiction & Recovery · I Ching · Buddha · Derrida · Chomsky · McLuhan · Jung · 1997: Lacan · Shakespeare · Structuralism

Dedications:

Kita Cá, who showed me the Gestalt path;
to **Mónica Nigro** and **Rosi Zupnik** for
their rapport all along the way;
to my companions at the **School of Gestalt** for
so much shared "awareness" among tears and laughs;
to **Jorge Genzone** for so much presence
and loving detachment;
to all Gestaltists whom I learned and learn with every day
("Learning is discovering", Perls says).

-Sergio Sinay

To **Elsa Lanza, Mónica Nigro**
and **Hernán Izurieta,**
with deep love and gratefulness.

-Pablo Blasberg

To the people who made and make the existence
of the **Buenos Aires Gestalt Association** (AGBA) possible.
- **Chía and J.C.K.** (for **Era Naciente**)

What are we talking about when we talk about Gestalt?
To begin with, we are using a word of German origin.
The term first appeared in 1523 in a translation from the Bible. Coming from a past participle (yor Augen gestelt), it meant something like: "put before the eyes, exposed to the looks".

Today many authors prefer to talk about Gestaltung: process of "taking shape" or "formation". They also agree that investigators Max Wertheimer (1880-1943), Kurt Koffka (1886-1941) and Wolfgang Kohler (1887-1967) were the first to turn this word into a theory.

Kohler was studying the behavior of superior primates.

Koffka was particularly interested in the relations between man and his medium.

KOHLER, KOFFKA AND WERTHEIMER were looking at psychologist **CHRISTIAN VON EHRENFELS** (1859-1932) who had said: **"THE WHOLE IS DIFFERENT FROM THE SUM OF THE PARTS".**

This was going to be a central idea of Gestalt, for it would demonstrate the fundamental importance of perception.

We are surrounded by sounds and forms that do not have a sole meaning. In a certain moment our perception is what—in that situation and that instant—gives it a meaningful and dominant form. For instance, what have we got here?

EUREKA! A CUBE!

Actually, we have got 12 lines: 4 horizontal, 4 vertical and 4 oblique. That is what is objective. The cube is born out of our imagination. We see 12 lines, relate them to our memory of a cube and our perception creates the figure. This form, figure, Gestalt or project emerges from a background, in this case from our subconscious.

Around 1912 Wertheimer, Koffka and Kohler presented a conjunct study that is considered as the foundation of Gestalt Psychology.

Gestalt Psychology was born drawing its inspiration from phenomenology. This philosophical school's father was Edmund Husserl (1859-1938), whose central idea was to describe and not explain phenomena. The phenomena that the psychologist founders perceived and studied were visual and audible figures always external from the subject.

One of the fundamental things those pioneers noticed was that in all perceptive fields (that is to say the field sensuously noticed) you distinguish a background and a form.

The **FORM** is a dominant figure that gets its meaning on emerging from the background...

The **BACKGROUND** is a rear plane that gives meaning to the figure or form ...

However, perception of the form is not an objective fact. The subject isolates the figure according to his attention and his needs.

Early Gestalt psychologists' works came to demonstrate that perception depends on objective and subjective interdependent factors, and that its relative importance could vary. Variation starts mainly from the subject, who—according to his relation with the medium—isolates the dominant forms from the background. In this way, the object's aspect depends on the needs of the subject.

Until Wertheimer, Kohler and Koffka set the basis of Gestalt Psychology (also called Psychology or Theory of the Form), psychology—established as a science in Germany between 1870 and 1880—considered the analysis of the mind's basic elements its main task.

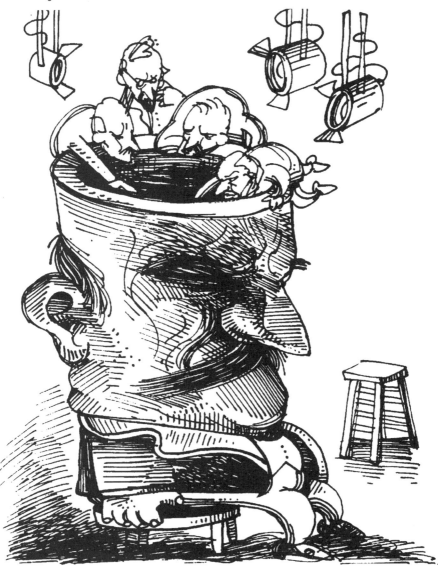

In that time two principal trends dominated the new science:

(A:) Watson's **CONDUCTISM** (or Behaviorism), that analyzed human behavior in terms of stimulus-response...

(B:) ...and **STRUCTURALISM**, of Titchener, Wundt and Ebbinghaus, that divided the subconscious into independent elements detached from values.

For Behaviorism the conscience did not exist and for Structuralism the whole (the conduct) was a simple sum of parts.

In 1914 a nationalist Serb killed Francis Ferdinand, archduke heir to Austria-Hungary, in Sarajevo. With this pretext quick alliances were formed and the "Great War" started, which lasted four years, produced 9 million casualties and changed the European map.
In 1912 (in an already convulsed climate), psychology had a confrontation of its own.

The creators of the new movement met at the University of Frankfurt and agreed that trying to understand existing phenomena (subject, object, medium) was no good unless they were seen as a complex whole, interdependent and interrelated.

Gestalt psychologists, who began studying perception, soon embraced other fields of research, such as learning, social behavior and thought. In time their basic formulas were introduced to all aspects of modern psychology.

In that time Sigmund Freud (1856-1939), Viennese neuro-pathologist physician, had already published *Studies on Hysteria* (1895), *The Interpretation of Dreams* (1900), *Psychoanalysis of Everyday Life* (1901), *Three Essays on the Theory of Sexuality* (1905), *Five Lessons on Psychoanalysis* (1910) and *Totem and Taboo* (1912).

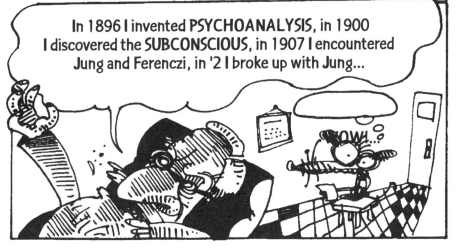

Foundations

Besides psychoanalysis, Gestalt Psychology would rub shoulders with expressionism (Friedlander), general semantics (Korzybski), transcendentalism (Emerson), psychodrama (Moreno). As we will later see, it would also combine with other very diverse currents...

WE'RE ALL GESTALTISTS...

Judaism   Zen Buddhism   Taoism

BUT DON'T THINK IT'S JUST A SIMPLE MEDLEY. NOW YOU'LL SEE HOW IT'S ABOUT A COHERENT ORIGINAL SYNTHESIS.

This is Claudio Naranjo, Chilean, one of the world's most respected current Gestaltists.

20 YEARS AGO, IN "GESTALT THERAPY TECHNIQUES", I SAID:

"Gestalt Therapy's building impresses us more than the old bricks that were utilized."

GESTALT THERAPY?

Is the Gestalt Therapy Naranjo talks about the same as Gestalt Psychology created by W., K. and K.? Not really: Carrying out a Gestalt basic, the whole is different from the sum of its parts. Gestalt Therapy does not arise, then, as a logical sequence following the Gestalt psychologists' studies.

¡¡◎#⚡⚡★✹!!

SO WHAT WE DID IS WORTH NOTHING?

Kohler, Wertheimer and Koffka were the trigger. Then came Bliuma Zeigarnik's contributions. In 1927, she came to the conclusion that an incomplete task demands twice as much energy and memorization as a concluded one...

HANS, YOU LOOK ABSENT-MINDED...

IT'S BECAUSE I'VE GOT MY HEAD ON THAT MATTER...

This kind of persistence was called "non-concluded Gestalt (or form)"

In those years, another German Gestalt psychologist, Kurt Goldstein (1878-1965), denies there is a dichotomy between the biological and psychical things and between the normal and the pathological ones...

DON'T LOOK ONLY AT MY BODY, BECAUSE EVERYONE IS A COMPLETE ENTITY (AND I'm not mad...)

This was known as "Global Theory"

Finally, also in that time (in 1922), Kurt Lewin (1890-1947), creator of group dynamics, formulated a solid and coherent theory about the relation between the individual and the environment...

This was called General Theory of the Psychic Field

Meanwhile, on the 8th of July 1893, in a Jewish Berlin ghetto, the third son of a somewhat strange couple was being born.

It was a long and difficult delivery...

...in which forceps had to be used...

The father of this baby was called Nathan, a wine fractionater and traveling salesman. He was also a Mason. The mother was called Amalia, an orthodox Jew, a stage and opera fan.

ELSE,
the older sister,
was blind.

GRETE,
the younger one, acted and
dressed like a boy.

Nathan and Amalia already had two daughters. The couple lived in an ambiance of hate, conflicts and constant fighting. Family life resulted in hell.

While he was growing up he was expelled from school...

...peeked under women's skirts...

...was severely punished by his parents.

His escapades did not end there: he forged his parents' signature in the school papers, was put as an apprentice in a sweets shop and failed, etc. He who was growing up in this way, apparently without destination, was called...

Friedrich Salomón

Perls

The Founder

Perls is considered the main founder of Gestalt Therapy. He was not a person with an easy life, as we have already been able to see by looking at his childhood. His personality too—generated to the beat of these and other episodes—was complex, ambiguous and controversial.

All those who knew and dealt with him seem to be somewhat right. However, Perls cannot be defined by only one of those adjectives, though none are strange to him...

THE THING IS, AS WE SAY IN GESTALT: THE WHOLE IS VERY DIFFERENT FROM THE SUM OF ITS PARTS!

Perls's adolescence was as turbulent and conflictive as his childhood. At 13 he was expelled from school. But the following year he showed some of the intuition that would accompany him all his life. He decided to apply on his own at another school...

And he met with a school fit to the needs and questions that were starting to emerge in him.

Perls's entrance to that school was particularly enriching for him. There he encountered the stage, an interest he would keep for life that would overflow in Gestalt Therapy.

His interest not only had to do with the artistic thing, but with what it offered as expression techniques. At school Perls met Max Reinhardt—famous expressionist director of the Deutsche Theater—and many other artists who lectured on total compromise...

When he finished school, young Fritz entered the University of Berlin to study medicine. In 1914 the war (remember we had announced it?) breaks out and he is excepted from the military service because of a heart malformation. In 1916 he went into the Red Cross as a volunteer.

On account of his being a Jew, he got the worst destinations, and even there he was persecuted and discriminated...

The war turned out to be a traumatic experience that lasted three years. In that time he was wounded in the head, exposed to mustard gas and saw all kinds of atrocities in the trenches...

It took him several years to recover from those episodes, and through-out that time he showed himself indifferent to everything.

Finally, at age 27 (on April 3, 1920) he graduated as a doctor in Medicine. Instead of spending his time at the hospitals, Perls dedicated it to cruising the Berlin cafés where the anarchist intellectual crowd hung out. There he would meet the people who were to influence him, among them the expressionist philosopher Salomon Friedlaender.

EXCUSE ME...AREN'T YOU THE AUTHOR OF "THE CREATIVE INDIFFERENCE" BY WHICH YOU OPPOSE KANT'S DUALISM?

Three years later Perls decided to travel to New York to revalidate his doctorate there. He was not able to do it because he did not know English. He went back to Germany frustrated and hurt (for the rest of his life) with the American culture.

In that time Perls was still living at his mother's, and the U.S. failure did nothing but emphasize the complexes that oppressed him...

On one of his hospital visits, he met Lucy, a woman older than him, with whom he had a passionate and torrid affair that made him break all his taboos.

That relationship was short. Perls felt excited, stimulated and guilty at the same time. His life went into a moving crisis, and he decided to submit himself to psychoanalysis. For that he chose Karen Horney (1885-1953), one of the most creative and profound personalities this century's psychology has produced. That encounter had a rich influence on him.

In 1927 Perls moved to Frankfurt. There he got a job as an assistant of Kurt Goldstein, who was working with people with brain lesions, using his experience of Gestalt psychology as the starting point. There Perls met Lore (who would later call herself Laura) Posner, a 21-year-old student.

You remember Goldstein rejected the dichotomy between biological and psychical things, between the abnormal and the normal, don't you?

Three years later Fritz and Laura got married. But before that, Perls analyzed himself for a year with Clara Happel, who abruptly interrupted the process and practically gave him an order:

GO AWAY TO VIENNA, FIND YOURSELF A SUPERVISOR AND BECOME A PSYCHOANALYST YOURSELF!

He was in Vienna for a year and had his first clients, supervised by Helene Deutsch (known as "the ice woman"). In 1928, back in Berlin, he was established as a psychoanalyst while he analyzed himself for a year and a half (five times a week!) with Hungarian Eugen Harnick, an ultraorthodox analyst who did not greet his patients and hardly ever uttered a phrase in an entire week. In 1929 Perls decided to marry Laura. Her family was against it. So was his shrink. Perls tried to finish with his analysis. Harnick later died in a hospital for mental disorders.

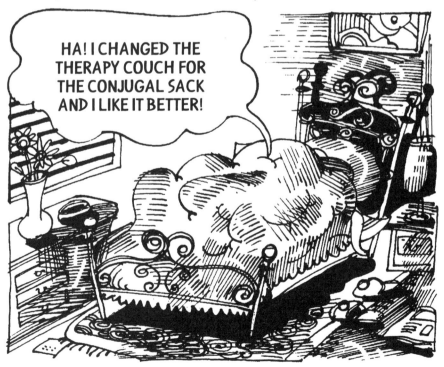

In 1930 Karen Horney suggested that Fritz analyze himself with Wilhelm Reich.

REICH was a vital, rebellious guy.... He was alive and I felt alive with him! We discussed everything, he was creative. I liked him so much!

Wilhelm Reich (1897-1957) was a precocious psychoanalyst—admitted at 23 in the Psychoanalytic Society of Vienna—who started as Freud's disciple and from 1924 to 1930 directed, by the latter's request, the psychotherapy technique seminary. In 1927 he published The Function of Orgasm, *where he attributes to orgasm a normalizing faculty that relaxes and harmonizes the energy in four times (tension, charge, discharge and repose). This, he says, marks the general law of life pulsation. After 1930 he broke with Freud and insisted more and more on the value of the present over the past's "archeology". Reich did active analysis: he touched his patients, included the corporal thing, worked with tensions and muscular armors. Besides, he related the aggressiveness, sexuality and politics in a direct way. He went beyond verbal speech; the how of phenomena mattered more to him than the why.*

Because of his heterodoxy and rebelliousness he was expelled from the Psychoanalytic Society of Vienna in 1933 and the International Psychoanalytic Association in 1934. He was also persecuted and imprisoned in the U.S. until his death. Reich deeply inspired Perls to create Gestalt Therapy.

In the meantime, far from healing, the wounds the war had left in Europe were becoming deeper. In Germany there was a somber atmosphere, of ominous omens...

Shortly after Hitler's ascension, and just when the persecution of the Jews grew stronger, Perls escaped with his family to Holland. It was 1933. In Amsterdam he was not granted a work permit. Then Ernst Jones—Freud's famous biographer, who helped many persecuted Jews—nominated Perls for a position as didactic analyst in Johannesburg, South Africa. Perls departed grateful and left a warning for his friends:

The journey lasted three weeks, and in that time Perls studied English. He was well received in South Africa. He soon had patients and founded the South African Psychotherapy Institute. Laura had graduated and was working as well. Many psychoanalysts began to study with Fritz. Steve, the second son, was born. The Perls became rich and famous.

Two years went by that were like a revenge in Perls's life. He was a rigid and orthodox therapist and a bon vivant. Berlin became a bad memory.

YOU'RE A MIXTURE OF A PROPHET AND A VAGABOND!

YOU'RE RIGHT, LAURA.

However, something started to worry him...

It would not be long before things started to change. In 1936 he was invited to the International Congress of Psychoanalysis in Prague, Czechoslovakia. He prepared a special work.

He had meant to contribute to the psychoanalytic theory, but his work was too revolutionary. And yet...

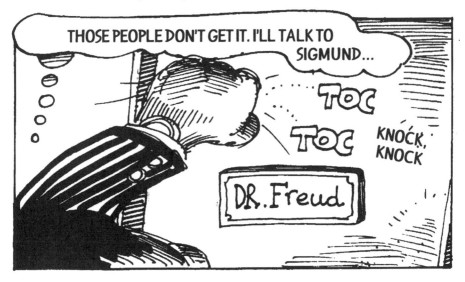

Starting from this moment Perls's rupture with Freud had begun. He thought he was going deep into the ideas of psychoanalysis's creator, but discovered he was on a path of his own.

In spite of his frustrations at the Congress (or thanks to them), 1936 was a decisive year. He got skeptical, mistrusted the scientific, political, philosophical and religious dogmas more, then denounced them...

He feverishly started to develop his own theses, discussed them profoundly with Laura, his main assistant, and in 1940 finished his first book, in which Laura wrote some chapters:

In the book several ideas emerged that would later culminate in Gestalt Therapy.

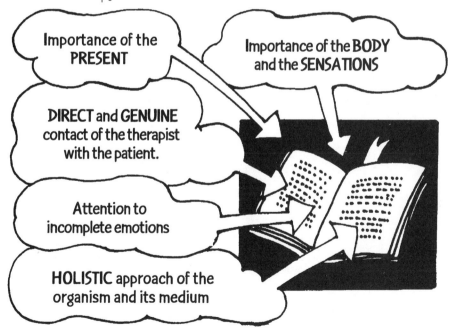

Importance of the PRESENT

Importance of the BODY and the SENSATIONS

DIRECT and GENUINE contact of the therapist with the patient.

Attention to incomplete emotions

HOLISTIC approach of the organism and its medium

Holism (based on ideas of Darwin, Bergson and Einstein) sustains that the organism is a mutual help society that, in turn, takes part in the medium. It is a whole that, in its present, holds its past and much of its future. The concept comes from Jan Christiaan Smuts (1870-1950), who was Prime Minister of South Africa and a founder of the United Nations. Perls admired Smuts.

In **Ego, Hunger and Agression** there were some ideas that turned Perls into a heretic for the psychoanalysts.

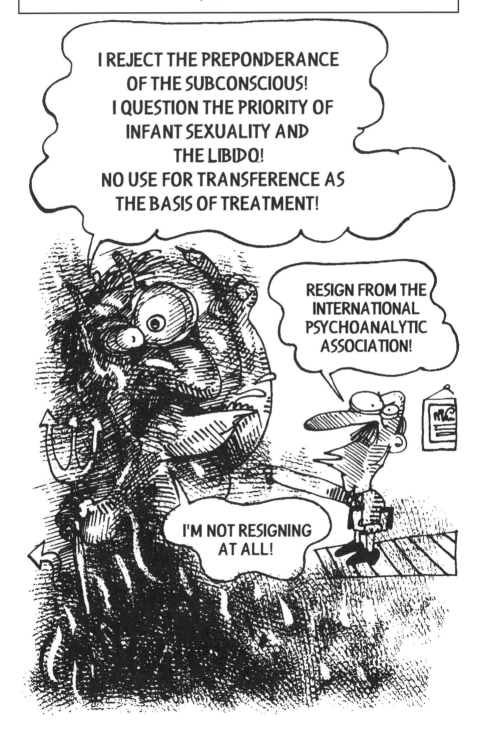

In those years he also studied the general semantics of Alfred Korzybski (1879-1959), who maintained that all experiences are multidimensional, meaning that what is emotional impacts on the intellectual and vice versa. Meanwhile, in 1942 (during World War II) he enlisted in the South African navy until 1946 as the corps psychiatrist.

Those four years of his life were full of conflict. He was absent from work, had affairs, was indifferent to Laura and ill-humored with his children, whom he sometimes punished as his father used to do with him.

In 1946 Perls made a decision: to move to New York. He left his family and luxurious house, and he departed.

In New York he was not well received. He was provocative, rebellious, anti-social, and he maintained his anti-Freudian positions that had already become unrenounceable...

In spite of everything, he soon had an abundant clientele, in part for his controversial attitudes and in part for the support of three important names in the field:

Though he continued using the couch, he believed less and less in this resource and what it implied. Instead, his attention toward group therapy was growing.

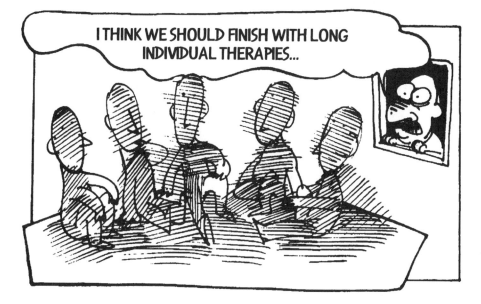

The bohemian and transgressive Perls revived in New York. He became a habitual personality in the artistic and intellectual ambiance, that proclaimed as he did the need to express feelings in a direct way and here and now. Among the people he then met were the poet and anarchist writer Paul Goodman and philosopher Isadore From. Both were to play leading roles in the events coming up. Meanwhile, in 1947, Laura and her sons arrived in the United States to live with him.

I NEVER LIKED THE AMERICAN CULTURE, BUT IN THOSE YEARS IT WAS FUNDAMENTAL FOR ME TO LIVE HERE, NOW YOU'LL SEE WHY...

The 50s started with the U.S. strengthened—after the war—as a power. In arts and sciences the country was enriched by the Europeans' contributions—immigrants with valuable knowledge and talents. In his turn, Perls had matured his own process and this was how...

...in 1950 the Group of the Seven was constituted, formed by Fritz and Laura Perls, Paul Goodman, Isadore From, Paul Weisz (psychotherapist who introduced Perls to the Zen), Elliot Shapiro, Sylvester Eastman and Ralph Hefferline (university professor). In 1951 the Group made known its first work: *Gestalt Therapy*.

Giving birth to this collective book was not easy. Discussion on the book title abounded.

Laura, who was Goldstein's student and had gotten her doctorate with a thesis on Gestalt Psychology, maintained her opposition...

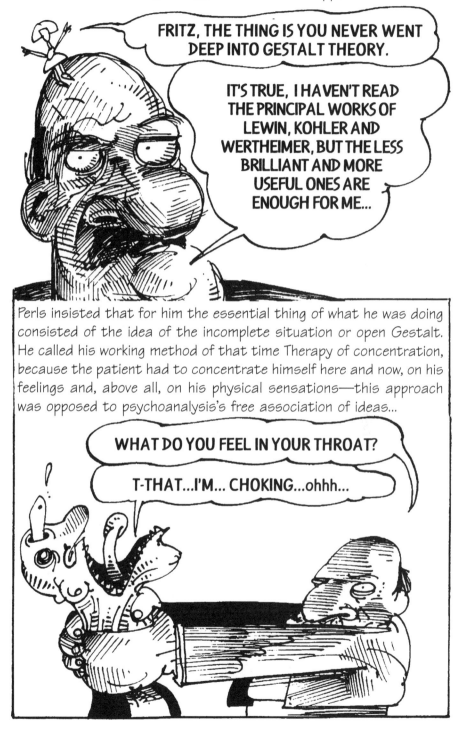

FRITZ, THE THING IS YOU NEVER WENT DEEP INTO GESTALT THEORY.

IT'S TRUE, I HAVEN'T READ THE PRINCIPAL WORKS OF LEWIN, KOHLER AND WERTHEIMER, BUT THE LESS BRILLIANT AND MORE USEFUL ONES ARE ENOUGH FOR ME...

Perls insisted that for him the essential thing of what he was doing consisted of the idea of the incomplete situation or open Gestalt. He called his working method of that time Therapy of concentration, because the patient had to concentrate himself here and now, on his feelings and, above all, on his physical sensations—this approach was opposed to psychoanalysis's free association of ideas...

WHAT DO YOU FEEL IN YOUR THROAT?

T-THAT...I'M... CHOKING...ohhh...

The fact is that, beyond the discussions, the book marked the official birth of Gestalt Therapy.

The four following years were vertiginous and prodigious for the newly-born practice...

In 1952 Fritz and Laura inaugurated the Gestalt Institute of New York.

In 1954 the Gestalt Institute of Cleveland was created.

Immediately Fritz left the institutes under the charge of Laura, Goodman and Weisz, and went on tour around the country to diffuse his THE method.

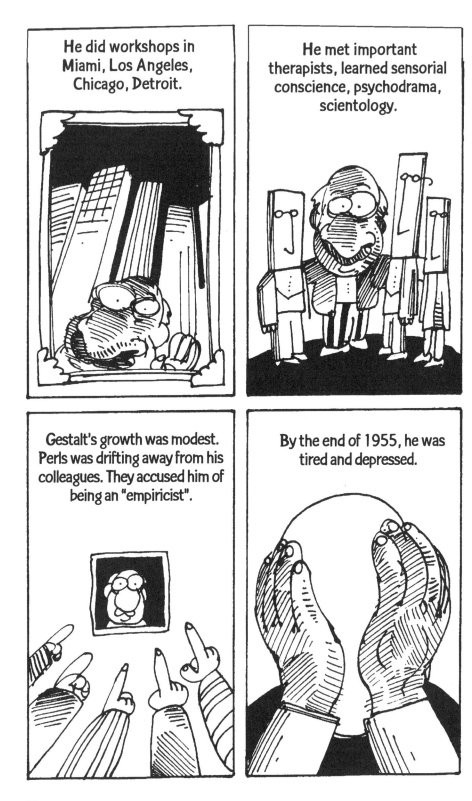

He did workshops in Miami, Los Angeles, Chicago, Detroit.

He met important therapists, learned sensorial conscience, psychodrama, scientology.

Gestalt's growth was modest. Perls was drifting away from his colleagues. They accused him of being an "empiricist".

By the end of 1955, he was tired and depressed.

All my life I've been depressive. It took me several days to come out of those downs...

He believed in nothing, did not love Laura anymore, and just dreamed about retiring to live in Miami.

I'M 63, CARDIAC, WHY SHOULD I GO ON?

He moved to Florida where he lived in a small dark apartment. He had some therapeutic groups and no friends. Until at the end of 1957...

I SWEAR SHE WAS THE MOST IMPORTANT WOMAN IN MY LIFE!

...he fell in love again, this time with Marty Fromm, a 32-year-old woman, shy and neurotic, who was preparing herself to become a therapist and who was his patient...

The love affair was intense, sexually boundless, lasted two years and in that period Marty did not divorce, even though she eventually would some time later. Together she and Fritz transgressed limits and taboos.

WITH FRITZ I LEARNED TO SHARE ALL FANTASIES AND FEELINGS, NEGATIVE OR POSITIVE, NOT TO PRETEND IN FRONT OF ANYONE AND TO GO RIGHT TO THE POINT.

BUT SHE DIDN'T WANT TO MARRY ME BECAUSE I WAS TOO OLD.....

In that time Perls tried LSD and hallucinogenic mushrooms, exploring his own paranoia and delirium....

I WANT TO EXPERIENCE MADNESS, I WANT TO REACH THE COSMIC CONSCIENCE.

Marty ended the relationship and, once more, it seemed as if the decline had come for Fritz. He could neither run away from his profession nor be a success. He clung to LSD, wandered...

Then two young Californian therapists appeared in his path: Jim Simkin and Wilson Van Dusen.

Simkin managed to convince him to quit drugs, and between him and Van Dusen—both admirers of Perls's therapeutic talent—they put him in touch with the most important psychotherapists of the time. In California Fritz was reborn as the Phoenix...

...and again he was surrounded by love and hate.

HE'S PATHOLOGICALLY JEALOUS

HE SEES EVERYBODY'S NATURE LIKE NO ONE ELSE.

THE THERAPY HE CREATED IS THE ONLY ONE THAT WORKS.

NOBODY USES THE BODY THING LIKE HIM

HE'S A LUSTFUL OLD MAN

HE'S THE TYPICAL MACHO CHAUVINIST

HE'S A VENERABLE MASTER

HE LIVES LIKES A PIG

Before turning 70, in 1962, he decided to go on a trip around the world that lasted eighteen months. He spent some time in Israel, where he was fascinated with the community life he came to know in a kibbutz (collective farm). In Japan he stayed two months in a Zen monastery searching for satori (illumination).

Back from the journey, on December 1963, he met writer Michael Murphy. He had inherited some beautiful land in Big Sur, California where, with his friend Richard Price, he had set up an institute and gave seminars and talks relating them to "The Great Vision".

A new way of life and of human relations. The Age of Aquarius was dawning with its new paradigms. Paul Tillich, Aldous Huxley, Arnold Toynbee, Norman Brown became venerated names. Murphy and Price wanted to turn the place (that had natural thermal springs) into a Human Potential Development Center, but—at first—it was just an attraction for bohemians, drunks, pot smokers...

Murphy invited Perls to join the experience, in spite of the fact that many considered him "an old crocodile waiting for death". They argued that Fritz didn't seem excited in spite of Murphy's background.

The place—that was on the coast, 150 miles south of San Francisco—was named after an Indian tribe that used to do its ceremonies there...

Finally, and reluctantly, Perls accepted a contract as a resident in Esalen. He started in April 1964 and, for more than a year, his disenchantment seemed to be deserved. He gave demonstration workshops and formation courses but there were no more than half a dozen people at each meeting. At 72, in 1965, he seemed finished again: his heart was worse than ever, he was so tired he could not even walk a block...

And then, believe it or not...he experienced a new resurrection!

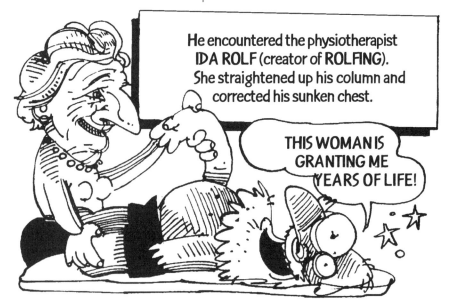

With renewed energy he went on with his therapeutic workshops, courses and groups. He built himself a beautiful house for his activities, that would later be famous. He began to write his memoirs ("Inside and Out of the Garbage Can")....

HIS WORKSHOPS BECAME MULTITUDINOUS. HE CALLED THEM "MY CIRCUS".

FRITZ

The 60s were coming to an end. Vietnam, Paris, Prague's spring, the sexual revolution, women's lib, the hippies, Woodstock... The world was living a time in which people were fed up and looking for new ways...

Now the climate was propitious for the flourishing of an existential approach like Gestalt Therapy. Perls was filmed and taped, his name was going around the country and the world, he started getting the acknowledgment and transcendence he had long been denied. His book *Dreams and Existence* (key work) was published, and then, at 75, he became a star of Humanist Therapies, which were proposing themselves as an alternative that was surpassing psychoanalysis. Big papers and magazines were busy with Perls and his proposals.

Esalen became what it would keep on being: a kind of Mecca for the new paradigms. The most brilliant representatives of the new therapies met and left their tracks there.

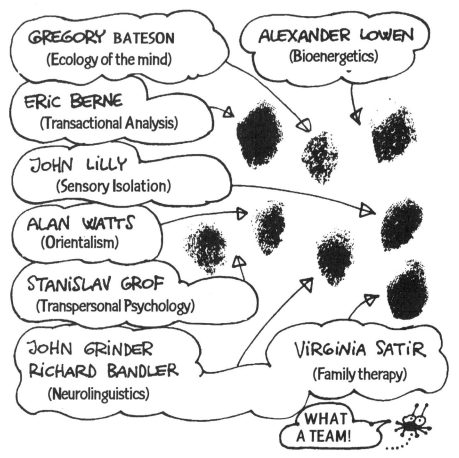

In broad euphoria and creative potency, Perls thought it was time to take one step further and put into practice a lifelong wish.

There, in June 1969, he founded a Gestalt Kibbutz, where he lived along with some thirty disciples from Esalen. There were collective chores, workshops, therapeutic groups, formative seminars. People from many places came to participate. There was only one requirement....

Like never before, Perls was happy, relaxed, energetic and creative. He was with the people that loved and admired him and would be his principal followers: John Stevens, Harvey Freedman, Barry Stevens, Jerry Rothstein, Virginia Horowitz, Abraham Levitzky, Stella Resnick, Ed Elkin, Richard Miller, etc.

At the beginning of 1970 he went on a pleasure tour to Berlin, Paris and London. When he departed, he expressed a sole desire:

Coming back from his journey he made a stop in Chicago, where he was invited to talk and coordinate some workshops. A myocardium infarct took him by surprise. He was taken to a clinic. He also suffered from pancreatic cancer. He died on March 14, 1970, shortly before turning 77. Laura was with him at the clinic. They had not lived together for 22 years, but he had never stopped consulting her.

Even after his death Perls remained an object of admiration and rejection:

According to his own wishes, Perls was cremated and then, in a ceremony at the San Francisco Civic Auditorium, 1500 people performed by the light of the candles a dance in celebration of life. It was a joyous celebration, just like he wanted.

And beyond the arguments between his followers or the questions of theorists or adherents from other trends, there was one conclusion on which all who had known him or entered into his work or practice agreed:

HE WAS THE CREATOR AND SPOKESMAN OF THE MOST IMPORTANT INNOVATION IN THE FIELD OF THERAPIES AND PERSONAL GROWTH SINCE THE MIDDLE OF THE CENTURY...

WHAT ARE WE TALKING ABOUT WHEN WE TALK....

Now we know the creator's story, a controversial, rich, nourishing, contradictory, lovable and incomprehensible character. All that, and more, at the same time. That is to say, a Human Being. We also know that Gestalt Therapy is not the same as Gestalt Psychology. Then what is Gestalt Therapy?

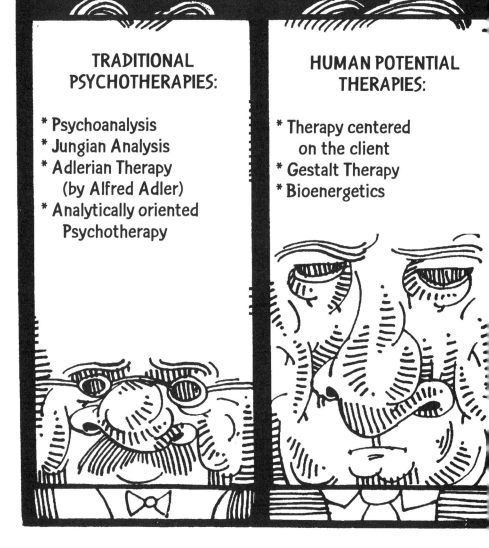

TRADITIONAL PSYCHOTHERAPIES:

* Psychoanalysis
* Jungian Analysis
* Adlerian Therapy
  (by Alfred Adler)
* Analytically oriented
  Psychotherapy

HUMAN POTENTIAL THERAPIES:

* Therapy centered
  on the client
* Gestalt Therapy
* Bioenergetics

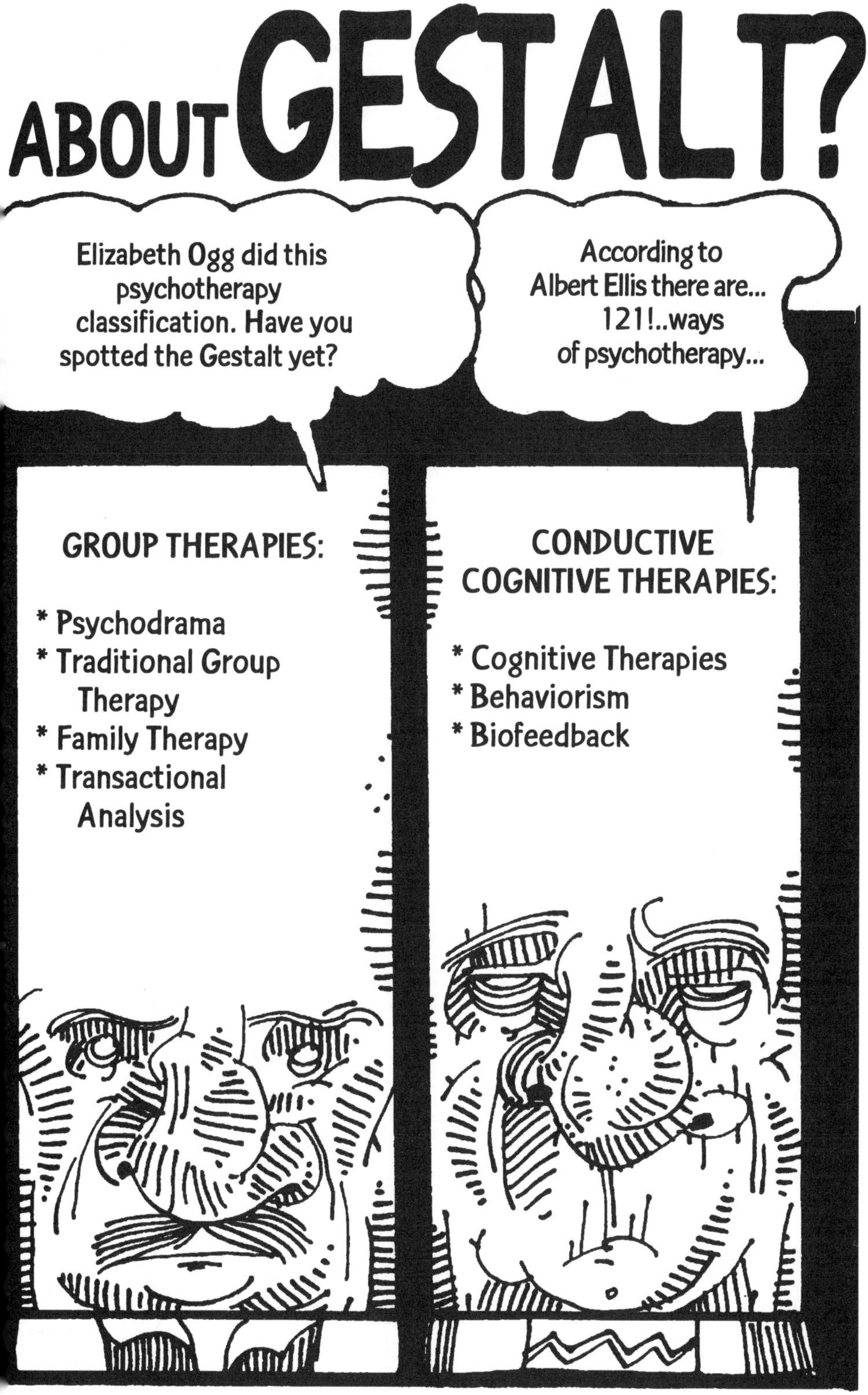

ABOUT GESTALT?

Elizabeth Ogg did this psychotherapy classification. Have you spotted the Gestalt yet?

According to Albert Ellis there are... 121!..ways of psychotherapy...

GROUP THERAPIES:

* Psychodrama
* Traditional Group Therapy
* Family Therapy
* Transactional Analysis

CONDUCTIVE COGNITIVE THERAPIES:

* Cognitive Therapies
* Behaviorism
* Biofeedback

From repressed sex to the Age of Aquarius

Another highly accepted classification—in this case chronological—is that of Ritchie Hering. It establishes the three great psychological schools of the century:

1 - The FREUDIAN or PSYCHOANALYTICAL
It was born in an era of sexual repression.

2 - The BEHAVIORIST- EXPERIMENTAL POSITIVIST
It appears before the half century, when the technological boom gives way to the "era of anxiety" and the therapies to modify behavior come forth.

3 - The EXISTENTIAL-HUMANIST or THIRD FORCE
It gathered strength in the last years of this century as a reaction to life's depersonalization and dehumanization. These therapies emphasize feeling (physiological and emotional, emotions, passion, immediate experience). They are centered in the present (moment of life in which we exist and feel). They form part of the appearance of the new scientific, philosophical, artistic, and political paradigms. Humanistic Psychology includes Abraham Maslow, Rollo May, Carl Rogers, Jacob Moreno, Alexander Lowen (Bioenergetics), Milton Erickson, Adlerians, Rankians (for Otto Rank), Jungians, Neo-Freudians, neo-Adlerians, post-Freudians (psychology of the ego), Marcuse, Gordon Allport, Kurt Goldstein's Organismic Psychology, etc., etc..

Humanistic Psychology said that orthodox psychoanalysis (with its focus on the family and social medium) as well as behaviorism (emphasizing cellular biochemistry) had reduced man to the status of an object to be studied, with no responsibility or possibility of growth. The movement came up with a different proposition.

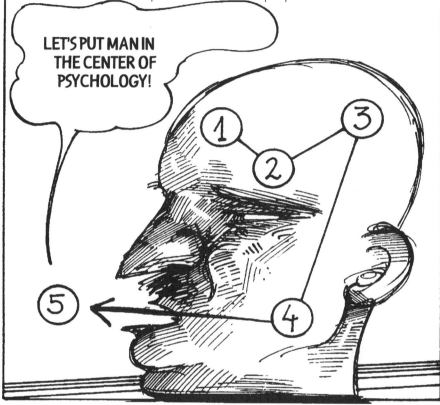

This trend was never organic, although it founded a magazine (*Journal of Humanistic Psychology*) run by Abraham Maslow, in order to gather and promote its approach. Today it includes diverse and therapeutic methods and approaches, recognized generally as Human Potential Movement. You could say it proposes to restore and respect man's dignity through the strengthening of three essential rights:

- the right to satisfy his needs, express his emotions, vindicate his feelings and value his body.
- the right to be different, unique and specific.
- the right to be fulfilled, to confirm his own individual, social and spiritual values, to not be limited by the will of others and not limit himself to "having" or "doing".

Humanistic Psychology leaves behind the dogmatic notions of health and disease, of "normal" and "pathological"

Refusing to build a wall between "existential malaise" and "disease", Humanistic Psychology parts from the premise that all human behaviors are normal. It places emphais on developing the individual's potential. It does not believe in cause-circumstance separation either; indeed, Man is an open global system, a system in itself that forms part of greater systems and organisms.

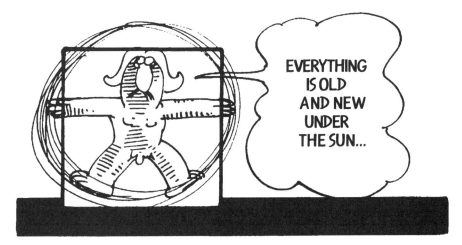

In this way Humanistic Psychology puts the accent on the new systemic and analogous paradigms, refusing other trends' reductionism. Perls insisted on one idea about the approach he had created:

Thus therapy does not necessarily appear to be related to sickness anymore. Therapy proceeds to be a tool for personal development.

Finally: is Gestalt a therapy? Perls's followers define it as something more than that.

Finally, Gestalt pursues an integrating holistic vision of being human, valuing a person's affective, intellectual, sensory, social, spiritual, emotional and physiological dimensions. For that it basically feeds on two currents:

It based these concepts on PHENOMENOLOGY:

From **existentialism**, Gestalt Therapy drew these notions:

Besides its contacts with phenomenology and existentialism, Gestalt Therapy has a close connection with currents of oriental thought. Perls, who had had some contact with Zen Buddhism, intensified it during his residence in Esalen. There he came into contact with Alan Watts, perhaps the main Tao exponent in the West (author of *The Way of the Tao*, among others). With Gia-Fu-Feng, who had just arrived from China, he came to know the essence of Tai Chi.

"Gestalt insists on the non-search, not on the find, on attention to the here-and-now and a healthy attitude in it. Besides, the Zen rests on the cult of attention and the acknowledgment of the perfection of the mind in natural state. Gestalt is a crypt Buddhism and a crypt Taoism. Taoism talks about the Tao of things and the Tao of individuals. This refers to a wise and deep spontaneity beyond the ego's conscious will. This is no different from the Gestalt ideal".

This is Claudio Naranjo. Remember him?

Contemporary physics has revolutionized concepts about matter, space, time, cause, effect. Picking up traditional oriental mystics' ideas, quantum scientists demonstrate that man is not apart from any of nature's phenomena.

In traditional science,
man is an observer.

In the new holistic vision (which includes Gestalt) man is a
participant and is committed.

A number of contemporary scientists base their theories on this vision: Fritjof Capra, Hubert Reeves, Jean Charon, Mitsuo Ishikawa, Olivier Costa de Beauregard, etc. We owe them the link between the Orient's millenary thought and the Occident's new paradigms. They start from a profound study of the Tao Te Ching, the book written by Lao Tsu in the fifth century BC. Known as the "Book of Life", it covers—through metaphors—the laws of nature and, above all, proposes non-intervention in the course of things.

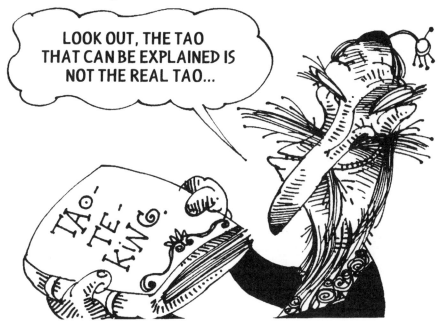

LOOK OUT, THE TAO THAT CAN BE EXPLAINED IS NOT THE REAL TAO...

The Tao maintains two essential and unavoidable principles:

The Yin (feminine) comprehends the beauty, the sweetness, the smoothness, the earth, the moon, the soft, etc. It is stability.
The Yang (masculine) includes the force, the penetration, the sky, the sun, the hard, the harsh, etc. It is movement.

The acknowledgment and integration of the opposite polarities is precisely one of Gestalt Therapy's main issues. Other questions Gestalt borrows from Taoism are:

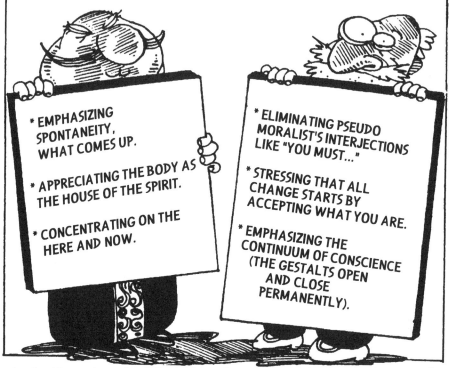

* EMPHASIZING SPONTANEITY, WHAT COMES UP.

* APPRECIATING THE BODY AS THE HOUSE OF THE SPIRIT.

* CONCENTRATING ON THE HERE AND NOW.

* ELIMINATING PSEUDO MORALIST'S INTERJECTIONS LIKE "YOU MUST..."

* STRESSING THAT ALL CHANGE STARTS BY ACCEPTING WHAT YOU ARE.

* EMPHASIZING THE CONTINUUM OF CONSCIENCE (THE GESTALTS OPEN AND CLOSE PERMANENTLY).

As for Zen, a branch of Buddhism that originated a hundred years after Taoism and reached Japan in the 12th Century, this current sustains that the awakening or illumination (called satori) comes after an alert wait, a vigil with no purpose. "There are no rules, no intentions in Nature, whatever is, is, whatever comes, comes".

IT'S WHAT THE GESTALTISTS CALL DETACHMENT, OR CYCLE OF CONTACT AND WITHDRAWAL. THAT IS TO SAY: "DON'T PUSH THE RIVER, LET IT RUN".

She is Barry Stevens, great disciple of Perls.

Zen and the Gestalt, however, have their differences:

Not to say a word about the couch

In the same way it has connections with oriental philosophies, Gestalt Therapy has connections with psychoanalysis as well, beyond Perls's rebelliousness against Freud.

I'M NOT DENYING THE UNCONSCIOUS, LIKE MY DEFAMERS SAY. I APPROACH IT THROUGH THE BODY, SENSATIONS AND EMOTION.

Neurosis—for Perls—is due not to "pseudo memories of childhood", or forbidden or repressed desires of the superego, but to a series of unfinished (interrupted and unsatisfied needs) Gestalts in a relation between the organism (the person) and his medium.

While in psychoanalysis acting-out is considered a resistance to verbalization, in Gestalt premature verbalization is taken as a resistance to letting the feeling act-out and the appearance of deep associative experiences.

For psychoanalysis, resistance is all that prevents the access to the unconscious. For Gestalt, resistance—more than a wall to tear down—is a potential creative energy in order to live in a difficult world.

Besides these differences, Gestalt owes something to great psychoanalysts such as:

Sandor Ferenczi.
(1873 - 1933)

Pampered disciple of Freud, he was underrated by the "hard" orthodox due to his pluralist contributions. He gave great importance to the body and to the therapist's subjectivity and personal style. He established the analysts' obligatory supervision. Fritz and Laura Perls went deep into a lot of his concepts.

Carl Gustav Jung.
(1875 - 1961)

Impeller of the humanist approach, he put the accent on the development of the self more than on the pathology. He proposed the therapist's active attitude and an intense relation with the patient. He prioritized the internal dialogue (interior drama) between the "personified" parts of the patient. He studied oriental philosophies, astrology and symbolism. Admired by Freud, Jung broke with him in 1912, following five years of hardships and deep arguments.

Gestalt finds certain things in common with other psychoanalysts:

MELANIE KLEIN (1892-1960). She gave importance to the corporal thing, introduced play therapy and observed the ambivalence (or polarities) love-hate and good object-bad object.

OTTO RANK (1834-1939). He reduced the duration of treatments, took elements from the dream as the dreamer's projections, impelled the therapy of creativity.

KAREN HORNEY (1885-1952). She again valued the importance of the cultural medium and that of the present, and rescued the secondary benefits of the patient's existential problems. She gave the sessions a warm and secure climate.

DONALD WINNICOTT (1896-1971). He gave play and creativity a preponderant place, recognized the value of the phenomenal and the necessities, reduced interpretation's relevance, and valued—like Horney—warmth and security.

Founder of the Gestalt School of Paris, author of *THE GESTALT: A THERAPY OF CONTACT*

According to Ginger's very creative synthesis, Gestalt would be in the center of a five point star. Each point indicates a way to the humane, and the different therapeutic approaches are situated in a section of the star.

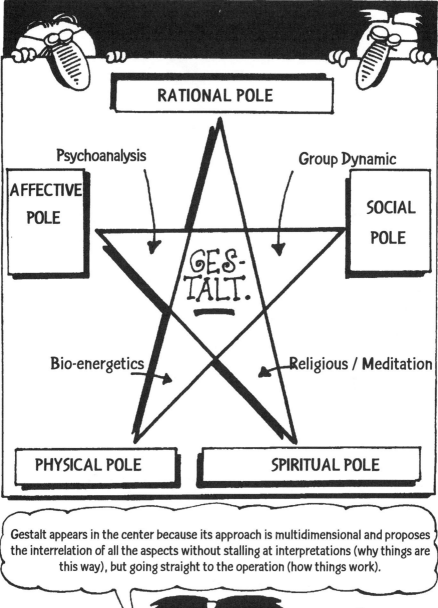

Gestalt appears in the center because its approach is multidimensional and proposes the interrelation of all the aspects without stalling at interpretations (why things are this way), but going straight to the operation (how things work).

The experiments, games, works, and representations that happen during Gestalt practice are not a series of empty techniques. Using a cushion is not to practice Gestalt. The techniques respond to a deep spirit that in turn feeds an approach to life. The techniques only make sense taken as a whole, and they depend on each therapist's singularity too.

The Gestalt techniques work from here and now and emphasize the sensations, with the goal that the patient may become aware of how he is preventing himself from fulfilling his needs and closing his Gestalts. They also consider the relationship I-you (patient-therapist) without impeding each one's independence and responsibility.

Awareness

It can be defined a deliberate consciousness about what is happening (physical sensations, feelings, imagination) "to me" and what is happening in the environment I am integrated in. Awareness comes from the answer to four key questions:

Awareness allows the patient to situate the therapeutic meeting; it is a warming up that also lets previous unfinished situations come out.

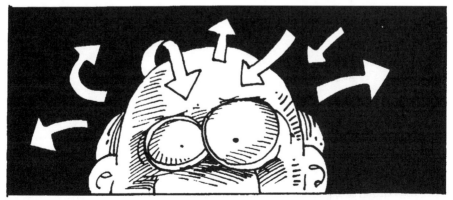

In turn, the therapist is attentive to his own flux of sensations and emotions. This is known as continuum of consciousness.

The "empty chair"

One of Perls's favorite techniques and one of Gestalt's "trademarks". In the "empty chair" (usually replaced with a cushion) the patient places any character of his life with whom he has an unfinished situation:

Used at the right time, the "empty chair" activates feelings and allows the patient to meet with unfinished characters or situations to see them here and now. Its exaggerated and discretionary use, however, can interfere in the direct contact between patient and therapist.

The "empty chair" also permits bringing into play a classic concept in Gestalt approach: the Top-dog and the Underdog. The first represents the person's desires, needs and potentials. The Underdog identifies the excuses, pretexts and obstacles the person puts in his own way. The Underdog may personify interjected characters.

The monodrama

This technique resides in asking the patient to play the different characters of an unfinished situation in his life, so as to have a clear experience of each one of them and their emotions...

Not only is it possible to represent other people, but it's also possible to represent the emotions, organs or emotions themselves.

Working on the representation of characters, emotions, abstractions or parts of oneself, the patient can clearly explore his polarities, get to know and accept them instead of reducing them to just one term. He can also register the differences and similarities with other people in his life. He is able to perceive that life manifests as a dynamic and changing balance.

Amplification or exaggeration

The therapist asks the patient to continue with some gesture or movement, to gradually intensify it and to exaggerate more every time. This increases the perception of certain mechanisms the patient uses in his contact with the environment to block his sensations and feelings...

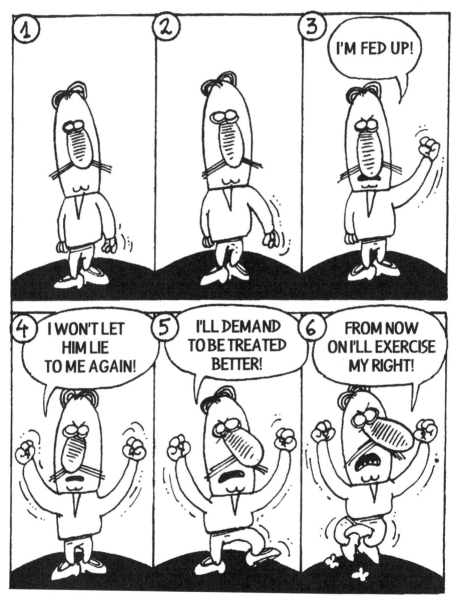

On amplifying his movement and his gesture and saying out loud what is the matter with him, the person hears himself, breaks the confused interior soliloquy. It becomes a revealing and modifying experience.

Talking "to" the other (direct interpellation)

This is essential in Gestalt work. The therapist discourages those phrases that, for not being directed to a specific addressee, prevent emotional contact.

Not to do "mind reading" is also part of the same question: this is to say, not projecting on the other your own feelings, wishes, fears, fantasies, etc.

Direct interpellation points to creating more direct contacts, without justifications, explanations, arguments, excuses or intents to convince. Contacts in which "what is" imposes itself on "as if" (what "should be"). This kind of dialogue requires honesty—the ability to say what you feel, think, want, and accept what you hear without judging it.

Talking in first person

This point is closely related to the other.

Gestalt maintains that the person is responsible for his acts, his thoughts, his feelings or emotions. They belong to him. When he talks in first person he becomes aware of all that he is, he exercises his responsibility. The contrary favors dissociation.

Dreams in Gestalt

Even though Freud appears as the first—in this century—to scientifically go deep into them, dreams have been, in humanity's history, a territory wherein answers, symbols, orientations are sought. The ways have been multiple, versatile, from esoteric to rational. Perls gave great importance to them in Gestalt Therapy. The big novelty that this therapy introduces is that dreams are not objects of interpretation or free association.

In *Gestalt Therapy Verbatim*, one of his fundamental works, Perls says:

"The dream is the most spontaneous expression in a human being's existence. In Gestalt Therapy we do not break up nor interpret dreams: we try to antedate them to life. We revive it as if it were happening now. We act it out in the present, so that it becomes part of one. Whenever it is possible to remember it, the dream will be alive and available and will contain an unfinished situation. In the dream we find the existential difficulty, the part that the personality lacks. Everything is there. The dream is an excellent opportunity to discover the personality's gaps. Understanding a dream means to have awareness of how much the obvious is being avoided".

In Gestalt a dream is worked starting from a description of each one of its elements.

Perls even suggested writing dreams down and enumerating the elements in writing.

The therapist may invite the patient to play out the dream's different elements talking as if he were each one of these elements. It is very important that this representation be not only verbal, but that the patient bring into play emotional and corporal resources as well so that he may feel and get the experience of each element. It is also possible to dramatize the dream.

"Each element of a dream is a part of ourselves. When I dream I write a script on my life, I say things about myself. Dreams can be seen as a camouflaged message. The message is existential, it is a message about how I exist, about the very nature of my existence".

Jim Simkin

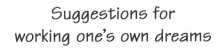

Suggestions for working one's own dreams

1) Tell the dream in first person and present tense, as if you were dreaming it now.

2) What part of the dream is less like you? Which part is it hardest to identify yourself with?

3) Go back to the dream and talk like that part, in first person and present.

4) Is the dream giving you any message? Is there anything about the dream that you recognize in you?

5) Once the dream has communicated its message to you, put it in the "empty chair" and express your gratefulness to it. If there is any other thing you want to say to it, do so.

Gestalt and the body

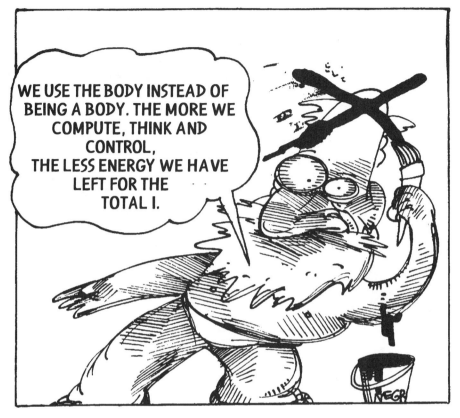

In Gestalt, voluntary and unconscious corporal manifestations, such as gestures, movements, micro gestures, tone of voice, postures, skin complexion, breathing are taken as important data of what is going on inside the patient. Body language is rooted in the here and now. The way to "awareness" that goes from the body to the word is followed progressively.

Gestalt Therapy goes farther than simple verbal acknowledgment of what is corporal (which does not bring into play what is emotional), and the mere emotional catharsis (which does not take what is corporal to a reflexive process). Gestalt enters into the interior processes of the body and in this way maintains consistency with its approach of the permanent relation background-form.

It is important to remember that mere movement or corporal agitation does not mean the Gestalt approach is being used. Appealing to the body has an objective, and results differ according to each specific group or individual situation, which may look for different "awareness" concerning experiences of abandon, tenderness, the enclosing feeling, trust, notion of limit, aggressiveness, etc., etc. This search is determined here and now, so the therapist is not able to rigidly program the "games" and "exercises" ahead of time. Corporal work—in Gestalt—does not push the flux of the therapeutic experience, but modulates along with it.

The results of this work are important to the body and the memory, too, for in the work it is possible to detect living materials from the pre-verbal infantile period, which cannot be accessed through purely verbal therapies.

Gestalt and the "awareness"

Gestalt techniques mainly aim at the patient's acquisition of conscience or awareness. This occurs when the person's organismic (that is to say, integral) attention is focused on a contact zone between the organism and the environment, where a complex interchange is produced that shows where a patient is blocked. In Gestalt it is said that something is going wrong when you are not conscious of that interaction's difficulty.

The Gestalt therapist does not intervene directly to make the patient conscious, but instead collaborates in restoring the conditions so that the patient, through the use of his capabilities, may have awareness and the events' natural flow can be restored.

The mechanisms by which people block becoming conscious of their own conduct are called resistance.

"These resistances prevent the individual from an adequate contact and balance between himself and the environment. They confuse the limit between the self and the other. This is how neurosis arises."

Resistance blocks the process of SELF-ACKNOWLEDGMENT and GROWTH

That is to say, it obstructs **self-support** and **maturity**.

Resistances—a fundamental concept in Gestalt—are several, though Perls considers four main ones:

1. Interjection

This is the mechanism through which a person incorporates, without digesting, all the information and mandates coming to him from the medium and acts according to them.

These unassimilated "alien bodies" are called interjects and impede the development and expression of the own self. By swallowing them without digesting them a person may find himself with two opposed or incompatible mandates working within him, and an attempt to reconcile them may contribute to personality disintegration.

WHEN THE INTERJECTOR SAYS "I THINK", IT MEANS "THEY THINK".

In the interjection the limit between the individual and the rest of the world shifts so much toward the individual that he almost disappears.

2. Projection

Interjection's the opposite side of the coin. In the projection the person ascribes to others the attributes he rejects about himself and shows himself absolutely critical, intolerant and hypersensitive towards these characteristics. He makes the environment responsible for what arises within him. He feels that everybody harasses him. He who is an introvert accuses others of being cold, etc. Pathology (of which paranoia is an extreme case) should not be confused with assumptions based on the observation of reality, which are normal and sane. So is the artist's projection when creating characters and stories.

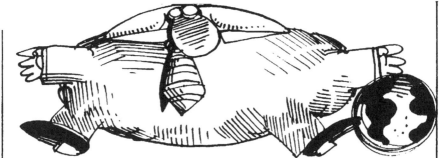

In projection the limit between the individual and the rest of the world is so shifted in the individual's favor that this one almost cannot detach himself from his attributes or have perspective.

3. Confluence

In this resistance the function of the ego is lost since the individual registers no limit between himself and the medium that surrounds him. The border between him and the medium is abolished. It is the state of a newborn child, natural in him, but not in an adult. The confluent lives confused, knows not what he wants, knows not what he feels, does not see the difference between himself and the rest of the world. He loses the sense of self. In the confluence, the habitual cycle of contact-retreat by which the individual maintains a healthy relationship with the medium does not happen. The confluent does not stand for either the differences or the confrontation.

In the confluence all notion or register of limit disappears. No difference is tolerated.

Everything has to be the same. It is the resistance of dictators, fundamentalists, sectarian groups or parents who consider their children as a simple extension of themselves.

WHEN THE CONFLUENT SAYS "WE" IT IS IMPOSSIBLE TO KNOW WHAT HE IS TALKING ABOUT.

Fritz Perls wrote a famous GESTALT ORATION, adopted by many and criticized by others, who see in it an excessive individualist or egotist. Beyond its various possible readings, some authors, like Ginger, see in ORATION a claim of the confluence:

"I do what I do,
you do what you do.
I did not come to this world to fulfill your expectations.
You did not come to fulfill mine.
I am I.
You are you.
If by chance we meet ourselves
it will be wonderful.
If not, there is no remedy".

4. Retroflection

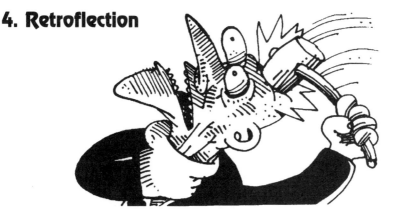

This mechanism is the one employed by people who do to themselves what they would like to do to other people or objects. The energies stop being directed toward the contact with the world to concentrate on the person's interior. In this ambiance he substitutes inside him the world in the place of his self. The retroflector invades his own interior world. A certain degree of retroflection is healthy, as long as it manifests as a reasonable self-control (Perls says this should not be confused with the Freudian superego). When it becomes a person's usual behavior, retroflection becomes a masochist inhibition of impulses or an exacerbation of narcissist manifestations. An example: the "altruist" or the "sacrificed" person who leaves everything behind for another.

The retroflector draws a very clear line that marks the limit between himself and the environment. But he draws it through the middle of his self. He sees himself and "his self" as two different things. He says "I'm ashamed of myself", "I owe it to myself", etc. He seems to be talking about two different people.

WHEN THE RETROFLECTOR TALKS "ABOUT HIMSELF", HE DOES NOT FEEL HE IS TALKING "ABOUT HIS SELF".

When retroflection becomes chronic it gives rise to diverse somatizations. The emotions and feelings dominated and turned toward themselves (what Laborit calls inhibition of the action) finally manifest as migraine, headaches, stomachaches, ulcers, etc.

Carl and Stephanie Simonton, known for their prestigious studies on cancer, observed that statistically the number of victims of this disease are people too in control, who manifest neither their negative emotions (grudge, rage, sadness) nor the positive (joy, enthusiasm, happiness). Retroflectors attack their own inmunological system.

The theme of confluence finally allows us to see another difference between Gestalt Therapy and Psychoanalysis.

Other mechanisms

Even though resistance is the most usual word, these mechanisms for avoiding contact—which may be sane or pathologic according to the intensity with which they are manifested—generally receive different names according to the approach of Gestaltists.

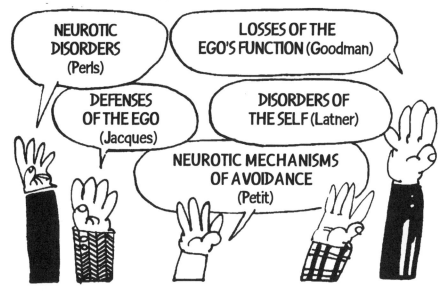

To the four main mechanisms, some Gestalt authors add others. For example:

Deflection

It is characterized by behaviors of avoidance, of deviation. The person does not involve or commit himself in anything and manipulates to avoid the exterior world. It is a category of Erwin and Miriam Polster.

Proflection

This conduct, described by Sylvia Crocker, combines projection with retroflection. It is about doing to another what we would like them to do to us.

Paul Goodman ascribed the label "egotism" to the mechanism by which an individual excessively develops a known ego (nationality, religion, profession, etc.) that risks annulling the rest.

Narcissism and hypertrophy of the ego relate to egotism. During a therapeutic process, there will be periods in which the patient manifests these attitudes, derived from the fact that he has begun to take care of himself.

There are therapists that, in Gestalt, consider egotism as a therapeutic tool for a time. That conduct, in a process of awareness, is gradually transformed into a transit—according to Jean Marie Robine—"from egology to ecology".

It is important to note that in Gestalt Therapy resistance is not meant to be beaten or "traversed".

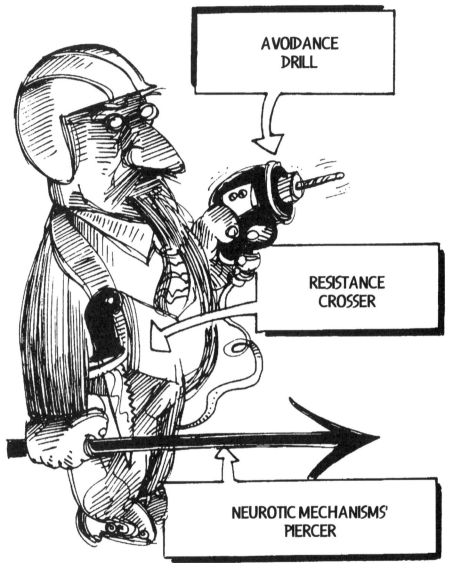

What the therapist does is point it out, so that the patient becomes aware of it. This acquisition of awareness allows adapting the mechanisms to the present situation (here and now). In Gestalt it is not forgotten that, under certain circumstances, "resistance" may operate as a necessary and healthy mechanism of accommodation. What transforms it into a prefixed neurotic mechanism is its appearance at inappropriate times and situations and its manifestation as the sole and rigid response in the cycle of contact and retreat.

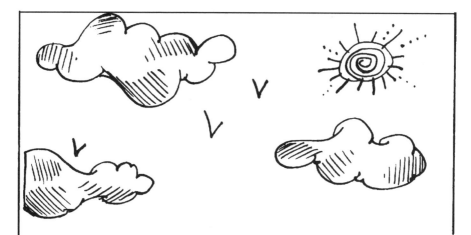

"All the organisms require an environment to exchange essential substances. We need the physical environment to exchange air, food, etc....We need the social environment to exchange friendship, love, anger...We always have to consider the part of the world in which we live as part of us".

—Fritz Perls

Neurosis, psychosis and health

Gestalt considers a healthy state to be one in which an organism (in this case, the person) has an internal equilibrium with the context he is in.

This equilibrium is the Homeostasis. The context, both physical and social, results in **transformation**. The equilibrium is transformed accordingly. The homeostatic process, says Perls, is one in which the organism maintains its balance, **and therefore its health**, in conditions that may vary. Finally, homeostasis is the process through which the organism satisfies its needs.

"So we arrive at the definition of health. It is an equilibrium, the coordination of what we are. I say *we are* and not *we have.* With *we have* we introduce a division: we say that *we have* an organism, *we have* a body. As if there were an *I* who possessed that body, that organism. This is not so. *We are* a body, *we are* somebody. The question is rather *to be* than *to have.* Now then, the environment also forms part of what we are. Wherever we go we take a kind of world along with us".

In normal conditions the organism registers a **necessity** (thirst, hunger, love, rage, light, company, etc., etc.) and moves into the environment to satisfy it. He comes into contact with the environment, satisfies the necessity and retreats. This is known as **Cycle of organic self-regulation, Cycle of experience, Cycle of contact-retreat** or **Cycle of the Gestalt** (a Gestalt is completed).

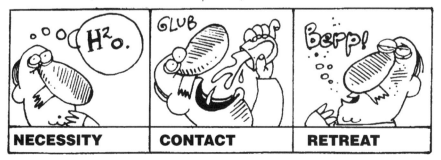

| NECESSITY | CONTACT | RETREAT |

NEUROSIS appears when the "it" perceives a necessity but the "I" does not give it an appropriate answer. Gestalt says that that answer is not updated: it is obsolete or anachronistic, responds to behaviors picked up at another time and place in life. The accumulation of these behaviors (of which resistance is an example) gives place to the neurotic disorder.

The creative adjustment of the behavior in consonance to the necessities is lost.

PSYCHOSIS is produced when the **perception** (capturing the world and the external stimulus) and the *properception* (capturing the world and the internal needs) are so disordered that there is no longer any adjustment between the subject and the environment. It is "out of reality".

According to the Gestaltists, the **self** of an individual is integrated in three **ways**:

It: includes the vital needs such as breathing, walking, sleeping, etc.— that is to say the automatic acts by which vital needs are satisfied.
It: is the active working by which contact with the medium is established, limiting or amplifying it according to one's own **responsibility**. It manifests starting from the acquisition of awares of needs and desires.
Personality: is the representation that the subject makes of himself, the image that allows him to recognize himself as responsible for what he feels or does. It integrates the previous livings and experiences and gives the feeling of identity.

How Gestalt Therapy works

In orthodox therapies the neurosis relates to a trauma that the individual "had" in the past. The objective of the treatment is to solve "that" problem. The whole approach aims at trying to capture that point in the past.

Instead, in the **Gestalt Approach,** the neurotic has a problem continuing **here and now**, in the present. The therapeutic objective is to get the patient into **awareness** about his avoidance mechanisms —that disturb his contact with the environment and the resolution of his necessities—in order to solve his **current** problem, as well as others that could arise in the future. It matters less if this problem exists **"because"** something happened in the past, than to notice how the person causes his own difficulties today.

Gestalt Therapy tries to give the patient the means so that he can solve his difficulties here and now. The fundamental tool for that is SELF-SUPPORT. This is strengthened to the extent that the individual gradually becomes aware at all times of his verbal, physical and fantasized actions. **Each resolved difficulty facilitates the solution of the next and increases self-support.**

For these reasons Gestalt is considered a **Here and Now Therapy**. It is also a **Therapy of Contact**. The patient is asked to pay attention to what he is doing at this moment, in the session, to be in contact with his gestures, his feelings, his sensations, the tone of his voice and his most urgent thoughts as well.

While he remains in the past, the patient acts and thinks as if he were still **"there and then"**, in those situations and with those characters determining his attitudes and guiding his life. He can talk about that, but the report is not enough to recuperate the living.

The Gestalt therapist invites him to abandon the mere report and transform his thought about the past into actions, into life experiences that may allow him to go through the past once more until he finds out the feelings and actions that were left interrupted. Gestalt does not believe in repressed desires or impulses, but in acts that were left interrupted.

In this therapy interpretations are carefully avoided...

...and instead it formulates questions that steer the patient to acquiring awareness of his own accord...

All the steps and techniques of Gestalt Therapy are aimed, it is emphasized, at producing **awareness**. Gestaltists believe that only when the individual becomes aware of what he does, of what happens to him, of how he does it or not, **is he able to realize what he IS and how he** is.

This marks an important moment of the therapeutic process. Once he shifts to awareness of how he is, the person can accept himself. Acceptance is an essential concept of Gestalt Therapy. Each organism is what it is...

"A rose....is a rose....is a rose." —**Gertrude Stein**

Acceptance as it is understood from the Gestalt approach is not resignation; **observing** permits the establishment of contact and proves cognition. Accepting that something or someone is what he is the only way of initiating change. And acceptance is, therapeutically, the first step in the consolidation of **Self-support**.

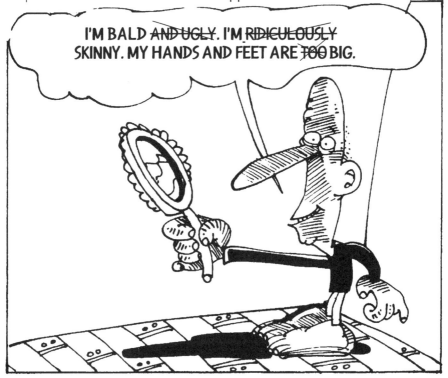

SELF-SUPPORT is the process by which the patient finds his own resources and solutions starting from acquring awareness of his behavior mechanisms and the development of his potentials.

This is an essential aspect of Gestalt Therapy. Usually the person who looks for a therapist wants to "change". Therapists who accept this generally establish what Perls called the dichotomy "of the oppressor and the oppressed".

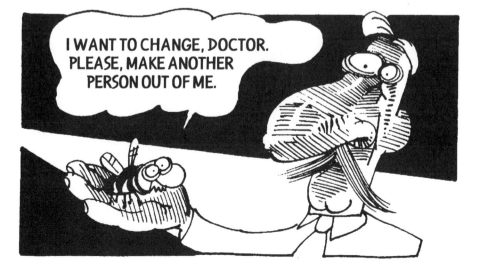

The Gestalt therapist supposes that in the patient two parts are in conflict and the demand to change is the voice of one of these parts.

By Gestalt Therapy's techniques and methods—and trying not to get involved in the dispute—the therapist hopes that, through this process, the patient becomes conscious of these aspects in conflict, that he fully experiments with what provokes him, that he identify himself with both parts and integrate them. **This acceptance and integration in themselves signify a change.**

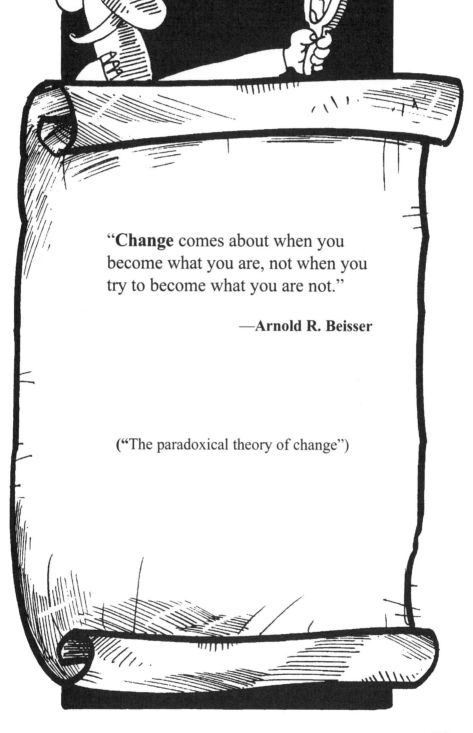

"**Change** comes about when you become what you are, not when you try to become what you are not."

—Arnold R. Beisser

("The paradoxical theory of change")

As the acquisition of awareness and the integration of its parts takes place, the individual leaves the cycle of **interrupted actions or unfinished Gestalts** that constitute his experience, and begins to discover his possibilities and expand his frontiers. He starts to make good contact with the world, based on his internal supports. He goes from...

EXTERNAL SUPPORT...

....TO SELF-SUPPORT

This is an essential objective of Gestalt Therapy: the transition from external support to self-support. This would be, in short, the person's maturity. Thus, by SELF-SUPPORT is understood the capacity that the individual has to take charge of himself, to satisfy his own needs, to move into the awareness that he is what he is in his here and now and, finally, to close his own interrupted Gestalts.

The role of the therapist in this process with patient is to **accompany**. It is important for him to understand prior to rationalization, to accept and not to feel obliged to act. Also to be **in contact,** that is to say attentive to what goes on with the patient, with himself (in his mind-body-spirit), in the environment and in the relation between both of them.

NOBODY TEACHES A PLANT TO GROW. IF I WATER AND CARE FOR HER, SHE GROWS ON HER OWN. THAT IS WHAT THERAPISTS DO.

The therapist is **present and active,** but not **directive** (he does not give instructions or "recipes"). As he encourages the patient to always talk in the first person, he himself remains attentive to his own sensations, feelings and thoughts and can even—deliberately—share some of them. Abraham Levitzky, direct disciple of Freud's, pointed out that, in a certain way, Gestalt is also a "therapy centered in the therapist".

You can say that the relationship between the therapist and the patient is established, in Gestalt, on three levels:

THE THERAPIST IN <u>EMPATHY</u> WITH THE PATIENT ("in him").

THE THERAPIST IN <u>CONGRUENCE</u> WITH HIMSELF ("in me").

BOTH <u>IN SYMPATHY</u> WITHIN AN I/YOU RELATIONSHIP
("between us").

Gestalt Therapy also seeks to prevent the patient from **transfering** characteristics of his own onto the therapist or from seeing him as a character from his "cast"...

In the same way, it tries to avoid the "positive" identifications (over-protective mother, "good breast", etc.) that lead to a patient's adhesion to the therapist for an unlimited time.

Sonia Nevis of the Gestalt Institute of Cleveland, designed a question-naire with 12 questions for the therapists in the making. The responses to the questionare give rise to the following synopsis:

General characteristics of the Gestalt therapist

- ✓ Ability to **say things in a precise**, brief, clear and direct **way.**
- ✓ Ability to **determine the "here and now"** and to remain in the present.
- ✓ **Sensor sensitivity** and corporal work.
- ✓ **Contact with own emotions** and ability to employ the acquisition of awareness directly and openly with others.
- ✓ Capacity to **discriminate between the phenomenological** (observed) **data** and the interpretation.
- ✓ **Awareness of his own intentions** (what he wants to say or do) and the ability to clearly make others see what he wants from them.
- ✓ To focus on the *continuum* of the process, to follow the path of experience, to **trust that something important will develop** and come to its close.
- ✓ Capacity to **be firm and gentle** in the same session.
- ✓ Ability to **accept and face emotional situations** himself and with others.
- ✓ Ability to show himself **in an attractive manner without imposing a charismatic presence.**
- ✓ Awareness of the **transcendental and creative points** of his work.

The Gestalt and the two hemispheres

Today it is known that even before birth, there is a difference between the two cerebral hemispheres in humans. The **left** one rules verbal, logical, analytic and scientific activities. The **right** relates to the spatial, analogous, synthetic and artistic functions. On the right are intuition, the emotions, fantasy, and the notion of time. It is said that people think with the left hemisphere and dream with the right.

According to this distribution of brain functions, it is possible to state that orthodox therapies adress the left hemisphere, while Gestalt Therapy attends to the right.

As long as this therapy works with corporal mobility, images, dreams and emotion it can be considered—much the same as those that integrate the corporal and emotional—as a **"psychotherapy of the right brain"**.

However, both hemispheres are connected, and quickly exchange information through the 200 million fibers that make up the body. They receive all the information—external and internal—at the same time and process it according to their characteristics.

It is known that the **left** hemisphere affects the contents of speech, inclines towards writing, provides a more organized and conscious thinking, allows one to remember people's names, emphasizes an optimistic character and sociability and grants a feeling of "I in the world".

The **right** hemisphere, instead, impels us to spare words, generates a systemic understanding of situations, awakens sensitivity to the sound and tone of a speaker's voice, allows us to recognize people by their faces (global Gestalt) and emphasizes the taciturn and pessimistic traits as well as the feeling of "The world in me".

A great part of the Gestalt techniques tend to encourage the participation of the right hemisphere to mobilize the emotion and allow a new approach to problems. Besides, as with an integrating therapy, Gestalt does not favor the annulment of one hemisphere in favor of the other, nor one's supremacy over the other, but the harmonious development of both potentials.

On stimulating the right hemisphere's participation, Gestalt Therapy also presents itself as a **creative psychotherapy.** Abraham Maslow placed creativity third among human needs.

According to Maslow, an essential part of any creative act is to "lose oneself in the present". His thought on creativity coincides a lot with Perls's...

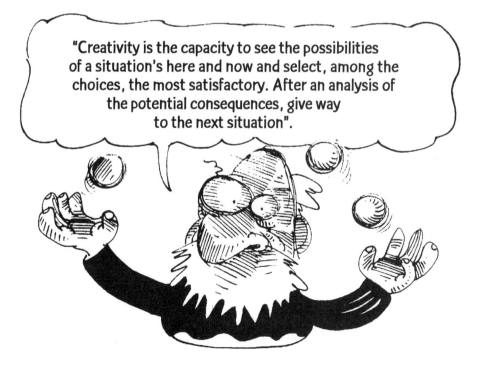

Joseph Zinker, a disciple of Perls's, was one of the first to study Gestalt Therapy as a creative process in which the therapist takes part.

The same Zinker, along with Sonia and Edwin Nevis, studies the factors that block the creativity of the patient, the therapist or a group and enumerates them in this way:

1. Rejection of risk
2. Rejection of play
3. Myopia before the resources
4. Excess of security
5. Avoidance of frustration
6. Life poor in fantasy
7. Excessive need of order
8. Reluctance to exercise influence
9. Resistance to "let yourself go"
10. Impoverished emotional life
11. Disintegration of the Yin-Yang
12. Numbness of the sensations
13. Subjection to customs
14. Fear of the unknown

"Our own growing is like a creative process in which we must abandon or rebuild certain forms of existence, and in the practice of freedom invent new forms or ways to experiment. To become creative we have to be free. Freedom is the consequence of *letting yourself be*. On passing from being fixed to letting ourselves be, we move from the mechanisms, from the religious rites, to the infinite experience of the self ".

—Joseph Zinker

"In the therapies with role play, dramatizations, etc..., the process of self-knowledge would be united to that of self-expression. In the context of the theatrical fiction or play therapy, the individual discovers that his role model is the origin of many problems (...) According to the point where each one is at, he must start out. The roads cross each other. For each one there are opportunities and encounters".
—Kita Cá and Elsa Lanza

Gestalt's territories

After Perls's death, Gestalt continued its geographic and social expansion. Geographically, it reached around the world. Socially the approach began to be applied gradually in more and more activities and situations.

From 1972 up to 1976, about **40 institutes of Gestalt qualification** were opened in the United States. Five years later—at the beginning of the 80s—**there were already more than 70.**

The Cleveland line puts its emphasis on the development of theory. Actually, most of the therapy's theorists were trained there. Those who identify themselves with the Cleveland current are the greatest producers of books and papers on Gestalt. They especially emphasize the study of the psychopathology, the psyche and the physiological processes as the therapist's nourishing elements.

As it developed, the Gestalt approach found its bearings in three great currents, generically known as **New York, Cleveland and California** In the New York or "East" branch (that also includes Boston) are counted the first and closest of Perls's disciples and comrades. In fact, he founded the first Gestalt institute in that city, in 1952. This school was distinguished, above all, by a verbal approach and it still maintained—by that way—bonds with psychoanalysis.

The California branch is rooted in the time Perls spent in Esalen, Big Sur, San Francisco and Los Angeles. In some way it includes the most spectacular and advanced expressions of Gestalt's practice. It privileges all those experiences where the emotional, the corporal and the spiritual have a decisive role. This current embodies "Gestalt's second foundation", produced when Perls found many of the original postulates obsolete, surrounded himself with new collaborators and faced new quests.

Among the principal names of the East branch are counted **Joel Latner, Paul Goodman, Isadore From.**
In Cleveland: **Laura Perls, Joseph Zinker, Edwin and Miriam Polster, Irma Shepherd.**
In the West: **Fritz Perls, Claudio Naranjo, Jim Simkin, Abraham Levitzky, Robert Hall, Gideon Schwarz, Jack Downing, John Enright.**

In any event, the trends have come together and fused due to internal moves and passes so that if there be any dispute it could be synthesized in this way:

The Eastern Gestaltists accused Perls of having become a "hippie" when he established himself in California, which took seriousness off the therapeutic approach. This argument continued in the controversy between the "theorists" (East) and "technicians" (West). According to the former, the latter only attended to techniques, without going deep into the theoretical bearings. From the West it is usually answered that the "theorists" tend to "fossilize" and "bureaucratize" the Gestalt face to the permanent flexibility, vitality and creativity.

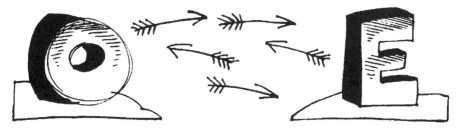

Claudio Naranjo (considered Perls's successor along with Hall and Downing) sustains that the important thing—above the theoretical "systematization"—"is the existential encounter the therapeutic relationship turns into." Rather than theory, he prefers to talk about the **spirit of the Gestalt**.

"That spirit is impossible to systematize because it escapes what is conceptual and practical, and has been transmitted through a transforming personal impact beyond professionalism".

—Claudio Naranjo

The Gestaltist's nearest to Perls's spirit maintain that the "hard-core" theorists try to set boundaries for Gestalt, which would lead to a bureaucratic stage, fossilizing it.

"Perls was interested in boundaries, but most of all to trespass them" says Naranjo.

In fact Gestalt Therapy transcended its initial geographical borders and extended itself throughout the world not only as a type of therapy but also as a holistic approach and a way of life. There are Gestalt qualification centers in Germany (the first was founded in 1972 in Dusseldorf), Australia, Mexico, Belgium, France, Canada, Japan (where the Gestalt Institute of Japan was started in 1978), Brazil, Spain, Mexico, Uruguay, Chile, and Argentina.

In the Hispanic world, Argentina and Chile produced pioneers in the Gestalt approach in the health, education and personal development fields. This happened at the beginning of the 70s. The first South American Gestaltists (except Naranjo, who emigrated to California in the mid-60s, after having introduced the first notions and experiences of the new current in his country) were trained with Dr. Adriana Schnacke, Chilean medical psychiatrist.

Known as **Nana** (or "the" Nana) , Dr. Schnacke oriented, already in 1970, her Psychiatry and Medical Psychology chairs at the University of Chile in a Gestaltic way.

General Pinochet's dictatorship—in which he raised all trace of creativity and humanism in the fields of culture, health, education, science—hindered the work of the Gestalt pioneers, though it did not impede the diffusion of its approach...

...and, paradoxically, contributed to turning Buenos Aires into the most important center of development for Gestalt Therapy. Here, in 1973 (year of the Chilean coup d'état), Nana did her first Laboratories of Gestalt Therapy and came into contact with psychologists, physicians and health care workers who would become her disciples and would later develop themselves as therapists, diffusers, investigators and teachers of the new current.

In 1976 the "process" (the sanguinary dictatorship that devastated territory, lives and institutions for seven years) darkened Argentina and forced the psychotherapeutic, research and educational or creative development activities into near clandestiness, but even still the Gestalt approach kept on growing and gaining followers.

In this way, by the end of the 70's the Gestalt Association of Buenos Aires (AGBA) was created, whose honorary chairman is Dr. Schnacke. Twenty years later, the approach of Gestalt Therapy in Argentina was extended to the education, the arts, the commercial field, medicine, and to multiple proposals for the development of human potential.

On account of this process, in June of 1995 Buenos Aires was the seat of the Sixth International Congress of Gestalt, organized by the AGBA.

Gestalt and its applications

Not just the geographical boundaries were transcended by Gestalt Therapy; the limiting conception that a therapeutic method can only be applied to the "cure" of a "disease" was too.

The practice and studies of the Gestaltists, from Perls on, placed a great deal of attention on the possibilities of this approach in the fields of health, especially in those situations and activities where people try to develop and integrate their potentials.

Gestalt is applied therapeutically in the treatment of psychotics, neurotics, psychosomatic patients, terminal patients, alcoholics, smokers, drug addicts, bulimics, anorexics, the depressed and suicidal, the sexually traumatized, phobic, etc., etc.

In addition, according to its integrating vision, Gestalt can associate its methods with those of other psychocorporal therapies: Bioenergetic, Transactional Analysis, Neurolinguistics Programming, Psychodrama, Rolfing, Yoga, Massages, Euthonia, Rebirth, Art Therapy, etc.

The Gestalt approach is applied, also, in numerous and varied institutions:

ASYLUMS

PRISONS

SCHOOLS

ARMIES

CHURCHES

HOSPITALS

TELEVISION AND
PUBLICITY

Marriage counseling and family therapy are two fields in which Gestalt proves highly efficacious.

The spirituality, the rites, the practices that explore the expansion of consciousness are other fields wherein this current makes fertile contributions and from where it, in turn, nourishes itself.

Because of its variety of resources and languages (verbal, corporal, metaphorical), Gestalt has great value in the social field. It enables the social worker to work in groups, individually, to observe the whole, the interaction between the individual and the environment...He is able to register himself in that relationship and direct his empathy, since in his function "objectivity" and "neutrality" are not possible and, often, are not desirable either.

To account for this plasticity and this richness of possibilities, we would have to examine—now that it is in perspective—the birth and conformation of this therapy, as well as the ideas and life experience of its creator. Gestalt Therapy can be adapted and re-created as we have seen because it is not about a rigid and unique formula that is applied to others, but something that is done **with** others. And they are always different, unique and non transferrable.

"Even though it is introduced as a specific kind of psychotherapy, Gestalt Therapy is based upon principles considered as a solid way of life. First it is a philosophy, a way of being, and starting from there arise the forms of employing this knowledge, so that others may benefit with it".

—Walter Kempler
(in *Gestalt Therapy*)

Almost a century has passed between the Theory of the Form's first manifestations and Gestalt Therapy's current flourishing. You can say that this process has been, in itself, Gestaltic: **it signified the development of a potential**

Here and now, these are some of the definitions of Gestalt:

"The Gestalt Therapy is a permit for being creative, a permit for playing with our most beautiful possibilities during our short life". —Joseph Zinker

"The Gestalt is: I and the universe are one, all my ego, the activities, the energy that surrounds me, the people and the things, all together we form a figure". —Joel Latner

Finally, at the end of this journey through the origin and development of a current that helped revolutionize and revitalize contemporaneous psychotherapies, we may ask ourselves: What path did Fritz Perls open with Gestalt? This is his answer:

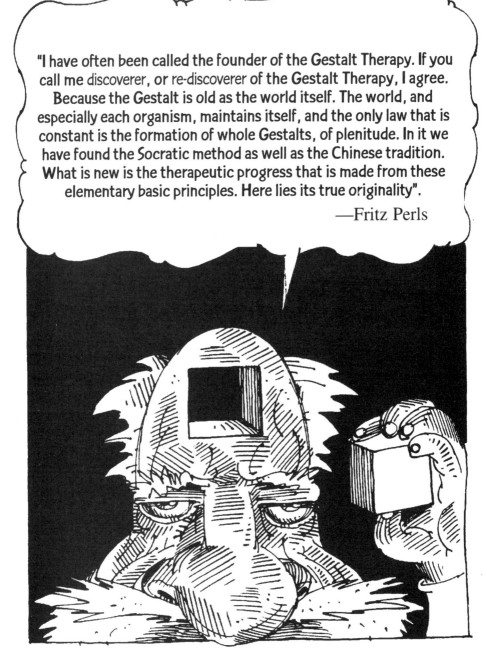

"I have often been called the founder of the Gestalt Therapy. If you call me discoverer, or re-discoverer of the Gestalt Therapy, I agree. Because the Gestalt is old as the world itself. The world, and especially each organism, maintains itself, and the only law that is constant is the formation of whole Gestalts, of plenitude. In it we have found the Socratic method as well as the Chinese tradition. What is new is the therapeutic progress that is made from these elementary basic principles. Here lies its true originality".

—Fritz Perls

To live in the way of the Gestalt
precepts enunciated by Claudio Naranjo

1. **Live now.** Concern yourself with the present before the past or the future.
2. **Live here**. Devote yourself to what is present before what is absent.
3. Stop imagining things. **Experiment with what is real**.
4. **Stop thinking unnecessary things**. Instead, taste and look.
5. **Express** instead of manipulating, explaining, justifying or judging.
6. Surrender yourself to distress and pain in the same way that you surrender to pleasure. **Do not limit your conscience.**
7. Accept no "you must" or "you should" other than the ones that you impose on yourself. **Do not adore any idol**.
8. **Accept being as you are**.

Brief dictionary of Gestalt

AGGRESSIVENESS: Fritz Perls considered it a life pulse, necessary to avoid interjections and actively assimilate the external world. "It is necessary to bite the apple so that you can digest it".

AMPLIFICATION: Technique that consists of progressively intensifying automatic gestures (a light rattling of the fingers, a jolt of the head, etc.), spontaneous feelings or sensations in order to make them explicit and to become aware of what is being avoided with them, what they stand for or what they are for.

ANGUISH: According to Perls, the gap that is opened between the now and the after. The paralysis of our vital energy when we wonder if our next action will be approved or rejected. The way of avoiding it is to stay in the present, since in the present the excitement flows towards the spontaneous activity in progress.

ASSERTION: A characteristic of language and behavior that affirms the self. It consists of defending and positing one's own feelings, sensations and needs in a direct way and without denying those of others.

ATTENTION: Attitude that leads to being in the present, conscious of one's own needs, sensations, feelings and mechanisms of contact. He who is attentive has awareness and takes charge of his acts. Attention puts us in a state of alertness about our own person and what surrounds us. It allows us to discriminate. According to Castaneda it is one of the four essential arms of the "Warrior" (wise man). For Gestalt attention is not something that "comes and goes", turns on and off, but is an attitude of life.

AWARENESS (Self-Awareness): Global acquisition of consciousness in the present moment. Meaning, attention to the ensemble of corporal and internal emotional processes and those of medium. Called awareness by Perls, it relates to an always subjective experience that does not go through that flow's intellectual comprehension. It is a total process, organismic, in which are situated all the answers a person can give on all possible fields of his conduct. It means awareness of one self, awareness of the world and awareness of the intermediate zone (of the fantasy). Unlike insight, it includes psychic and physical behaviors. Latner defines awareness as "a final aspect of the healthy working of the individual, it means grasping with all the senses the internal and external phenomenological world, just as it is and happens." He who is in awareness can only be so in the present moment, in contact with what at that moment is emerging as figure. Therefore, he has awareness of the whole Gestaltic field.

CHARACTER: For Perls, a rigid structure of behavior. It is the "callosity" that is produced in the frontier-contact of the individual and the medium, resulting in little creativity and flexibility in the interaction. A person of "character" is, actually, someone with a poor variety of answers to different stimulus or necessities, poorness that makes him predictable.

CONFLICT: Situation that results when two internal forces (in Gestalt, generally the top-dog and the underdog) are in struggle. Many of Gestalt Therapy's techniques teach the individual to discriminate between these forces, identify himself with each of them, get them to talk, and find the point from where they interact. The basic conflict appears, say Gestaltists, when a person does not accept himself as he is.

CONFLUENCE: Mechanism of resistance by which the frontier of contact between an individual and the medium becomes diluted so that the individual does not notice or tolerate any difference between him and the rest of the world. The confluence in a baby (with his mother) is normal; in an adult it is pathologic.

CONTACT: One of Gestalt's central ideas. It designates the relationship between the individual and the world. Contact and retreat are two moments that open and close the cycle of an experience that defines any action taken for the satisfaction of an identified need. Goodman describes four phases in this cycle (pre-contact, contact, full contact and retreat). Other authors find more phases, as does Katzeff, who describes seven. What is sure is that the cycle of experience, once completed, closes a Gestalt and, once it's completed, allows a healthy and harmonic relationship between the person and the context. The interruptions or alterations of this cycle (projection, interjection, confluence, retroflection and deflection) are called **resistances** and are considered **neurotic disorders**. Each one of them displaces the frontier and spaces of the individual and the environment.

CONTINUUM OF CONSCIOUSNESS: State of alertness about one's own perceptions, sensations, feelings and ideas while these remain as **background** for the **figures** that emerge and catch our interest. It is about a constant conscience on the internal world that in a healthy person appears like a regular and flexible flow. In a Gestaltic therapist it is an essential resource.

DEFLECTION: Resistance by which an individual avoids contact, deviating or making the interaction bounce back to the intermediate zone so as not to come into contact with unwanted situations or people. The deflector uses the energy to avoid being centered in himself, runs away from the here and now by way of general issues, projects, day dreams, jokes, trivial conversations. Perls called this "mind fucking".

DIALOGUE: Technique that is used in Gestalt Therapy to seek the integration of parts in conflict. It is used in cases where a dissociation is observed in the individual: he is made to experiment taking each of the parts in conflict and talking or acting them out. He can also be made to dialogue with a person for him who is absent but important to him, asking him to identify with that person. The dialogue can be established between different parts of the body (left hand with right hand, brain with heart, etc).

EMPTY CHAIR: Technique preferred by Perls, who used it especially from 1964. It consists of asking the patient to install himself in front of an empty seat and imagine a character (for example, his father) that he needs to talk to. The "empty chair" may be a cushion and it can be put in a variety of places in accordance with where the patient places it.

ENCOUNTER: Contact between the person and the medium, between two people, or between parts of a person that produces a modification or change in the structure of those that contact each other. There are no ways or formulas to make this happen. It happens or not, although it does not occur by chance; one prepare's the conditions so that the encounter be possible. For this it is necessary to dislodge the intermediate zone— fantasy, opinions, prejudices, expectancies, intentions, etc. and to intensify attention and alertness.

EXPERIENCE: The ensemble of knowledge that a person obtains about himself through attention, alertness and awareness of his mechanisms and ways of contact. The experience occurs in the here and now and can be verified not only in the mind, but also by sensory, emotional and affective ways.

EXPERIMENT: Situation in which the individual is deliberately asked to live, feel, try (that is to say, experience) of his own accord—and generally in a symbolic way—a feared or expected situation. This is meant to avoid escape from distressing situations. Zinker calls the experiment "the cornerstone of learning through experience. It transforms talking about something into a doing, and stale reminiscences and theories into being completely here, with the imagination, the energy and the interest".

EXTERNAL SUPPORT: Substitutes for self-support that are obtained from mechanisms of manipulation. These mechanisms go from self-pity ("Poor me, who cannot do it on his own...") to flattery ("Only you can help me out....") to the veiled threat ("I'm telling you this for your own good...") among others.

FIGURE-FORM: Basic concept of Gestalt Therapy, taken by Perls from the psychology of perception. It basically defines the fact that when a person's attention is focused on something this turns to **figure** and everything else passes to a second plane working as **background.** A healthy person has the ability to discern the dominant figure in the here and now (the registering of a necessity, the perception of what is needed to satisfy it and the necessary action to obtain it). In this way an action reaction in the here and now (figure) is inserted in the whole of the personality's situation (background). When the necessity has been satisfied, the open or unfinished Gestalt is closed, the figure retreats to the background and from this one emerges a new figure. This continuous and changing succession is no more than the cycle of life and within it all living organism's are engaged.

FORM: In Gestalt, equivalent to signification and opposed to significant (content). It basically relates to the how (tone of voice, expressions, gestures, postures, etc.) and is especially important in the therapeutic process.

FRONTIER-CONTACT: (SEE CONTACT): Fundamental concept in Gestalt, since it is in the individual's frontier-contact with the environment where the therapy takes place. The skin is, in the organism's way, the clearest example of this notion.

GESTALT: Word of German origin that means *whole* or *configuration*. Not only does it relate to the configuration itself, but particularly to the way in which the individual parts that comprise it are organized. The psychology of Gestalt parts from the premise that human nature is organized in forms and totalities and that this is how the individual experiences it. Thus, human nature can only be understood according to the forms or totalities it is composed of. Gestalt is then the whole process that includes actions, emotions and thoughts that flow from the appearance of a necessity to its satisfaction. Perls says: "When the catexial object, whether his catexis is positive or negative, has been appropriated or annihilated, contacted or moved away, or treated in some way that is satisfactory for the individual, then the object as well as the necessity with which it is related disappear from the environment and it is said that the **Gestalt is closed**." An **open Gestalt** is an unsatisfied necessity or an unfinished matter and while it remains this way it impedes the appearance of new Gestalt, complicating the continuum of the **cycle of the experience**.

HEALTH: Characteristic of an individual who can live alert in the here and now, feeling without rejecting his feelings, making himself responsible for them and for his action, without being subjected to apparitions of the past or being anxious to control the future. The healthy man is one who can have significant contact with his medium without being totally absorbed by it and without withdrawing himself completely from it. It is what Perls calls "the well integrated man". Perls proposes: **"The target of the psychotherapy is precisely to create these kind of men."**

HERE AND NOW: The sensations, life experiences, sensory experience, contact that describe a situation in the moment in which it happens. It relates to a continuous state of present. Meaning, according to Deshimaru, "being entirely into what you are doing and not thinking in the past nor the future".

HOLISM: From the Greek "holos", which means *all*. It makes reference to the relation of the part with the whole. The holistic theory was posed by General Smuts, prime minister of South Africa, in his book *Holism and Evolution* (1926). Perls came to know it and was seduced by it when he lived in that country, in exile from Nazi persecution. Smuts developed the theory starting from ideas of Darwin, Bergson, Einstein and Teilhard de Chardin. Holism developed and gathered strength as a response to the dogmatism of the theories that assert that only the body or only the mind is important. Holism maintains that separation of mind and body constitutes the basic weakness of traditional psychotherapies. The currents partaking of the psychotherapeutic Third Wave, of which Gestalt Therapy forms part, are **holistic**. Perls points out: "The organism acts and reacts to the organism with more or less intensity; as the intensity grows, it becomes physical behavior (...) Once it is recognized that the thoughts and actions are made of the same energy, we can translate them and transpose them from one level to another".

HOMEOSTASIS: General principle of the **self regulation of living organisms**. The homeostatic process is the one by which the organism maintains its equilibrium—and therefore its health—in the midst of changing conditions. That is to say, it is about the process through which the organism satisfies its necessities. Needs are constant and varied, so that each one of them alters the balance and obliges it to be rebuilt. Homeostasis is, therefore, a phenomenon of unsteady balance, which occurs all the time. Cannon first enunciated this principle, in 1926. For the homeostasis to be accomplished, the individual has to have the capacity to register his necessity and to know how to manage himself and his environment in quest of its satisfaction.

HOW: Essential question in Gestalt Therapy, that fundamentally relates to the phenomenological perspective of the processes. In personal relations this question is facilitating, for it allows one to get true information and impedes the judging and the chain of always relative interpretations triggered by the search of the "why".

IMPASSE: Psychic block or paralyzing situation, apparently with no way out, that is produced when, according to Perls, you are at the "nucleus" of the problem. It arises when, in the course of the therapeutic process the patient gets close to a phobic point. Then he generally falls into repetitions, refuses to go on, and all his mechanisms of avoidance arise. The way out is to adopt new paths that should gradually allow crossing—from outside to inside—the successive layers of neurotic conduct to touch the most authentic layers. This generally comes with emotional outbursts that break the block.

INTEGRATION: Process by which a projection comes to be accepted as one's own. The individual stops acting from only one of his personality's opposed poles to recuperate an alienated, devaluated aspect placed "outside". The way to integration is by getting to the bottom of a sensation or feeling, being responsible for one's own feelings, thoughts, words and actions.

INTERJECTION: A basic resistance, that consists of accepting—without metabolizing—all the ideas, principles or dogmas of others without personalizing them. The interjectors follow to the letter, for instance, all the **you shoulds** that are imparted.

INTERRUPTION: Consequence of neurotic behavior, which cuts the flux of energy at any part of the cycle of experience and impedes reestablishment of the homeostatic balance.

IT: For Gestalt, one of the three functions of the self, which also contains the **I** and the **personality**.

LABORATORY: One of Gestalt Therapy's most used techniques, consisting of group work aimed at living in the here and now, through experiments, the true contact of each participant with himself and with others.

LEARNING: Learning is discovering, says Perls. There is no other effective way to learn. "You can tell a child a thousand times that the stove is hot, but it is no good: he has to discover it for himself." Learning comes as a consequence of carrying out the cycle of experience. When this is interrupted, a gestalt remains unfinished and there is something that is not learned. When it is necessary to think, you think here and now, remember here and now. My autobiography belongs to the past. My projects to the future. The succession of here and now becomes cosmic and extends to the infinity." Perls prefers the "now and how", that describes the development of the interaction, in the present, with another.

MATURITY: According to Perls, thiscomes as a consequence of the trans-formation from environmental support to self-support. Is the objective of Gestalt Therapy: to complete this process to succeed in that the individual may not depend on others, but will soon discover that he is able to do many more things than he imagined.

MONODRAMA: Technique coming from psychodrama and utilized many times in Gestalt. It consists of making the patient represent different roles within the situation that he evokes. In this way he can talk with different parts of his body or people in his life and give himself the imagined, desired or feared answers.

NECESSITY: An impulse whose results are impossible to elude. Unlike desire, necessity designates the lack of something that is indispensable for subsistence. That lack signifies a risk or danger that demands quick help. Necessities can be organic, psychological, social or spiritual and are not always quickly perceived or expressed. Gestalt pays attention to necessities above desires, while the therapeutic process aims at indicating the interruptions, blocks or distortions (**resistance**) that interrupt or disturb the **cycle of satisfaction of the necessities**.

NEUROSIS: It is defined in Gestalt as a state of rupture of the homeostatic equilibrium in the individual, that appears when a person and the group or environment of which he forms part experience different necessities and the person cannot determine which is the dominant. The repetition of this experience obliges the individual to see himself disturbed enough to lose the capacity of properly judging the state of balance or unbalance of any situation. "The neurotic is not able to see his own necessities clearly and so is not able to satisfy them". (Perls)

OBVIOUS: It is what can be captured by the senses. Gestalt Therapy lays special stress on not confusing what is obvious with what the person imagines, believes to see or "takes for granted or known". Due to resistance it usually happens that the obvious is just what is less seen.

POLARITIES: Characteristics of human behavior (love-hate, aggressiveness-tenderness, reason-intuition, courage-fear, etc., etc.) whose harmonious integration is Gestalt's objective. Gestalt does not pursue the elimination of one in favor of the other, nor the finding of the "exact mean" (both illusory and impoverishing); it pursues complementation.

PROJECTION: Form of resistance that consists of attributing to someone else an aspect of oneself. Paranoia is an extreme form of this objects and people in the environment. His conviction that he is being pursued is, actually, the confirmation that he would want to pursue others. "Instead of being an active participant of his own life, the projector becomes a passive object, victim of the circumstances:"

RESISTANCE: Fundamental concept in Gestalt Therapy. It designates those mechanisms of behavior that, by dint of repetition, are opposed to the free development of the cycle of contact or satisfaction of necessities. Perls defines four basic resistances (or "mechanisms of disorder of the contact's limits"): interjection, projection, confluence and retroflection. Other authors add others (like deflection, proflection, egotism, etc.)

RESPONSIBILITY: Ability or capacity to find the answer to one's own necessities and take charge of oneself. Responsibility signifies **responsa-habil** (skillful response). The exercise of responsibility is one by which we become aware of our emotions, feelings, thoughts, words and actions and take charge of them—not in the style of taking the blame, but as an acknowledgment of their existence. The responsibility is not centered on what a person feels, since this arises spontaneously in him, but on what that person does with what he feels. Responsibility means talking in the first person. The **"I"**, Perls points out, develops the individual's sense about his own feelings, thoughts and symptoms. The **"am"** is an existential symbol. "It mentions what he experiences as forming part of his self, that along with his now, is his getting to be. He rapidly learns that each new **now** is different from the previous one".

RETROFLECTION: Resistance consisting of turning mobilizing energy against yourself, or doing to yourself what you wish to do to others. The retroflector substitutes the environment for himself and succeeds in becoming his own worst enemy.

SELF-ACTIVATION: Model according to which there is a continuum that goes from manipulation to activation. The manipulator sees others as ends and acts accordingly, controlling himself and the others. For the activator the other is an end in himself and before the other expresses emotions and feelings the moment they arise. Attention and awareness lead to staying self-activated. Perls points out: "A lot of people dedicate their life to activating (updating) a concept of what they should be, instead of activating themselves as they are. This difference between being self-activated and activating the self-image is very important."

SELF-SUPPORT: The person's capacity to take charge of himself starting from the acceptance and acknowledgment of his potentials. Self-support defines the ability to be aware of one's own needs here and now and to satisfy them, so completing a Gestalt.

SUBCONSCIOUS: Even though Gestalt does not deny them, it does not attribute to the phenomena of the subconscious the main role in the therapeutic process. Gestalt Therapy inverts traditional psychotherapy's way and goes from the apparent or most superficial (corporal, emotional or mental) manifestations to the deepest layers.

TOP-DOG AND UNDERDOG: Perls's denominations. The Top-dog is what in psychoanalysis is known as the Superego (and also conscience). "Full of virtues, he is exemplary and authoritarian, always right", Perls describes him. "He is a bully and works with **you should and you should not.** He moves about with demands and threats of catastrophes such as if you do not yield you will not be loved, you will not go to heaven, you will die and that sort of thing". The top-dog is always normative. He is right and clear. Psychoanalysis, Perls points out, forgot about the underdog, who is as real as the one on top. The underdog says yes to everything, "I promise you", "I agree", "I'll do it tomorrow if I can". He is defensive, apologetic, flattering, he plays the weeping baby. He is clever and astute, says Perls, and in general gets the better part because he is more manipulating and less primitive than the one on top. Both dogs fight for control of the person and fragment him into controller-controlled. The internal conflict that they motorize does not solve why both fight for their lives. "If the person sets his mind on accomplishing the top-dog's perfectionist expectancies, the result will be a nervous breakdown or an escape to psychosis. This is one of the underdog's tools." Perls adds that the way to solve this struggle between "the two nasty clowns" is to gain awareness of one's conduct, recognize it and get to understand that the point of reconciliation is to abandon all pretense of internal or external control and let the situation be the one to control. "The less trust we have in ourselves, the less contact with ourselves and the world, the greater our desire to control". Anyway, the conflict never disappears (the resolution of one makes room for the appearance of another), even though placing oneself in the center of the battlefield permits one to visualize both poles and reach acceptance.

Index

THE AUTHORS

Sergio Sinay

Writer and journalist. He was born in Buenos Aires in 1947. He published four novels and four non-fiction books, the most recent **"Esta noche no, querida"** (in English, **"Not Tonight, Dear"**), **"Inolvidable: el libro del bolero y el amor"** (**"Unforgettable: the book of the *bolero* and love"**) and **"Hombres en la dulce espera"** (**"Men in tender expectancy"**). He coordinates masculine identity and writing groups. Editor of **Persona** magazine, he won the Essay Prize of **La Nación** newspaper, of Buenos Aires. His works have been translated into Portuguese and French. He graduated from the Postgraduate School of the Gestalt Asociation of Buenos Aires, where he was trained in the Gestaltic approach and techniques.

Pablo Blasberg

He was born in Buenos Aires in 1970. Ever since he was very young he has worked as an illustrator for the main Argentine papers and publishers (Clarín, La Nación, Atlántida, Perfil, La Urraca). He won the Second Prize in the contest of Clarín for illustrators and caricaturists (1988) and the First Prize in the Biannual of Young Art (Illustrated Humor) 1991. As a flute player he integrated a variety of orchestras (among them, the Latin-American Musical Youth and the Juvenile of Radio Nacional) and classical music ensembles, and gave concerts in the country and abroad.

How to get original thinkers to come to your home...

Orders:

U.K

For trade and credit card orders please contact our distributor:

Littlehampton Book Services Ltd, 10-14 Eldon Way, Littlehampton, West Sussex, BN17 7HE
Phone Orders: 01903 828800
Fax Orders: 01903 828802
E-mail Orders:
orders@lbsltd.co.uk

Individual Orders: Please fill out the coupon below and send cheque or money order to:
Writers and Readers Ltd., 35 Britannia Row, London N1 8QH
Phone: 0171 226 3377
Fax: 0171 359 4554

U.S.

Please fill out the coupon below and send cheque or money order to:
Writers and Readers Publishing, P.O. Box 461 Village Station, New York NY 10014
Phone: (212) 982-3158
Fax: (212) 777 4924

Catalogue:

Or contact us for a FREE CATALOGUE of all our For beginners titles

Name: _ _ _ _ _ _ _ _ _ _ _ _ _ _

_ _ _ _ _ _ _ _ _ _ _ _ _ _ _ _ _ _

Address: _ _ _ _ _ _ _ _ _ _ _ _ _

_ _ _ _ _ _ _ _ _ _ _ _ _ _ _ _ _ _

City: _ _ _ _ _ _ _ _ _ _ _ _ _ _ _

_ _ _ _ _ _ _ _ _ _ _ _ _ _ _ _ _ _

Postcode _ _ _ _ _ _ _ _ _ _ _ _

Tel: _ _ _ _ _ _ _ _ _ _ _ _ _ _ _ _

Access/ Visa/ Mastercard/ American Express /Switch (circle one)

A/C No: _ _ _ _ _ _ _ _ _ _ _ _ _ _

Expires: _ _ _ _ _ _ _ _ _ _ _ _ _ _

ADDICTION & RECOVERY (£7.99)	HISTORY OF CLOWNS (£7.99)
ADLER (£7.99)	I CHING (£7.99)
AFRICAN HISTORY (£7.99)	JAZZ (£7.99)
ARABS & ISRAEL (£7.99)	JEWISH HOLOCAUST (£7.99)
ARCHITECTURE (£7.99)	JUDAISM (£7.99)
BABIES (£7.99)	JUNG (£7.99)
BENJAMIN (£7.99)	KIERKEGAARD (£7.99)
BIOLOGY (£7.99)	KRISHNAMURTI (£7.99)
BLACK HISTORY (£7.99)	LACAN (£7.99)
BLACK HOLOCAUST (£7.99)	MALCOLM X (£7.99)
BLACK PANTHERS (£7.99)	MAO (£7.99)
BLACK WOMEN (£7.99)	MARILYN (£7.99)
BODY (£7.99)	MARTIAL ARTS (£7.99)
BRECHT (£7.99)	MCLUHAN (£7.99)
BUDDHA (£7.99)	MILES DAVIS (£7.99)
CASATNEDA (£7.99)	NIETZSCHE (£7.99)
CHE (£7.99)	OPERA (£7.99)
CHOMSKY (£7.99)	PAN-AFRICANISM (£7.99)
CLASSICAL MUSIC (£7.99)	PHILOSOPHY (£7.99)
COMPUTERS (£7.99)	PLATO (£7.99)
THE HISTORY OF CINEMA (£9.99)	POSTMODERNISM (£7.99)
DERRIDA (£7.99)	STRUCTURALISM&
DNA (£7.99)	POSTSTRUCTURALISM (£7.99)
DOMESTIC VIOLENCE (£7.99)	PSYCHIATRY (£7.99)
THE HISTORY OF EASTERN EUROPE (£7.99)	RAINFORESTS (£7.99)
ELVIS (£7.99)	SAI BABA (£7.99)
ENGLISH LANGUAGE (£7.99)	SARTRE (£7.99)
EROTICA (£7.99)	SAUSSURE (£7.99)
FANON (£7.99)	SCOTLAND (£7.99)
FOOD (£7.99)	SEX (£7.99)
FOUCAULT (£7.99)	SHAKESPEARE (£7.99)
FREUD (£7.99)	STANISLAVSKI (£7.99)
GESTALT (£7.99)	UNICEF (£7.99)
HEALTH CARE (£7.99)	UNITED NATIONS (£7.99)
HEIDEGGER (£7.99)	US CONSTITUTION (£7.99)
HEMINGWAY (£7.99)	WORLD WAR II (£7.99)
ISLAM (£7.99)	ZEN (£7.99)

Individual Order Form (clip out or copy complete page)

Book title	Quantity	Amount
	SUB TOTAL:	
U.S. only — N.Y. RESIDENTS ADD 8 1/4 SALES TAX:		
Shipping & Handling ($3.00 for the first book; £.60 for each additional book):		
	TOTAL	

GESTALT FOR BEGINNERS ™
Sergio Sinay
Illustrated by Pable Blasberg
Translated by Mariana Solanet
ISBN 0-86316-258-4
(UK £7.99)

The origins of Gestalt Therapy derive from several sources, such as psychoanalysis by way of Wilhelm Reich and experimental Gestalt psychologists studying the nature of visual perception. It also includes field theorists such as Lewin and Humanist-Existential ideas that come primarily through the work of philosopher Martin Buber.

Gestalt, a German word with no exact equivalent in English, is usually translated as *form* or *shape*. Gestalt Therapy takes an holistic approach to healing and personal growth. It is a form of experiential

psychology that focuses on elements of the *here* and *now*. What we experience as we develop and how we adapt to that experience, come into the present as unresolved problems.

The purpose of Gestalt therapy is to teach people to work through and complete unresolved problems. Clients learn to follow their own ongoing process and to fully experience, accept and appreciate their complete selves.

Gestalt For Beginners ™ details the birth of the therapy, investigates the complex life of its creator Fitz Peris, and describes his revolutionary techniques such as the **Empty Chair**, the **Monodrama**, and the **Dream Studies**. The author also demonstrates why Gestalt Therapy is an ideal approach to self-affirmation and personal growth.

SAI BABA FOR BEGINNERS ™
Marcelo Berenstein
Illustrated by Miguel Angel Scenna
Translated by Mariana Solanet
ISBN 0-86316-257-6
(UK £7.99)

120million devotees worldwide recognise Sathya Sai Baba as a modern Hindu *avatr* (a human incarnation of the dicine) with the ability to be in various places simultaneously and with absolute knbowledge.

Why does this man claim to be God? Who gave him that title? And what did he come here for? **Sai Baba For Beginners** ™

details Sai Baba's life from his birth in 1926 to his studies, miracles, works, programme of education in human valor and his messages, up to the celebration of his recent 70th Birthday.

s new?

**THE HISTORY OF
CINEMA FOR
BEGINNERS ™**
Jarek Kupść
BN 0-86316-275-4
(UK £9.99)

The History of Cinema for Beginners™ is an informative introductory text on the history of narrative film and a reference guide for those who seek basic information on interesting movies. The book spans over one hundred years of film history, beginning with events leading up to the invention of the medium and chronicles the early struggle of the pioneers.

Readers are introduced to people behind and in front of the camera and presented with all major achievements of the silent and sound periods - even the most intangible film theories are explained and made easily digestible.

The unique aspect of **The History of Cinema For Beginners™** is its global approach to the subject of film history. The author introduces the reader to such significant developments as the Soviet montage, Italian neorealism, the French New Wave, the British kitchen sink cinema and the New German Film while providing a comprehensive coverage of American genre films such as slapstick comedy, the western, film noir, and science-fiction.

In addition, **The History of Cinema For Beginners™** invites the reader to delve into the lesser known regions of World cinema: Eastern Europe, South-East Asia, South America and others. The book also presents every key figure in the vast world of cinema with detailed information on his or her background, technique and major accomplishments. In a lighthearted manner, film makers such as D.W. Griffiths, Sergei Eisenstein and Orson Welles present their unique approach to movie making. The book's main goal is to make learning about movies as entertaining as it is watching them.

**STMODERNISM FOR
BEGINNERS ™**
Jim Powell
ustrated by Joe Lee
3N 0-86316-188-X
(U.K. £7.99)

If you are like most people, you're not sure what Postmodernism is. And if this were like most books on the subject, it probably wouldn't tell you.

Besides what a few grumpy critics claim, Postmodernism is not a bunch of meaningless intellectual mind games. On the contrary, it is a reaction to the most profound spiritual and philosophical crises of our time -- the failure of the Enlightenment.

Jim Powell takes the position that Postmodernism is a series of *maps* that help people find their way through a changing world. **Postmodernism For Beginners** features the thoughts of Foucault on power and knowledge, Jameson on mapping the postmodern, Baudrillard on the media, Harvey on time-space compression, Derrida on deconstruction, and Deleuze and Guattari on rhizomes. The book also discusses postmodern artifacts such as Madonna, cyberpunk sci-fi, Buddhist ecology and teledildonics.

THE BODY FOR BEGINNERS ™
Dani Cavallaro.
Illustrated by Carline Vago
ISBN 0-86316-266-5
(U.K. £7.99)

What is the body? Is it a natural object? An idea? A word?

The Body For Beginners ™ addresses these and other questions by examining different aspects of the body in a variety of cultural situations. It argues that in recent years the body has been radically re-thought by both science and philosophy. Science has shown that it can be disassembled and restructured. Philosophy has challenged the traditional superiority of the mind over the body by stressing that corporeality is central to our experience and knowledge of the world.

Exploring the part played by the body in society, philosophy, the visual field and cyberculture and drawing examples from literature, cinema and popular culture, mythology and the visual arts, **The Body For Beginners** ™ suggests that there is no single way of defining the body. There are eating

bodies, clothed bodies, sexual, erotic and pornographic bodies, medical bodies, technobodies, grotesque and hybrid bodies, tabooed, cannibalistic and vampiric bodies - to mention just a few of the aspects considered in this book.

No one map of the body is valid for all cultures. The word *body* will always mean something different, depending on the context in which it is used. This implies that the body can no longer be seen as a purely natural entity. In fact, it is a construct produced through various media, especially language.

All societies create images of the ideal body to define themselves. Framing the body is a vital means of establishing structures of power, knowledge, meaning and desire.
Yet, the body has a knack of breaking the frame. Its boundaries often turn out to be unstable. And this instability can be both scary and stimulating at the same time. This book will appeal to you if you are curious about the body as something more exciting and multi-faceted than simply a lump of meat!

s new?

ENJAMIN FOR BEGINNERS ™
Written and illustrated by
Lloyd Spencer
ISBN 0-86316-262-2
(U.K. £7.99)

november 1998

Benjamin For Beginners ™ offers a clear accessible guide to one of the most intriguing and inspiring thinkers of the 20th century. Since his suicide in 1940, the ideas of Walter Benjamin have influenced contemporary writers like Jacques Derrida, Paul de Man, George Steiner, John Berger and Terry Eagleton. Today, Benjamin's essays are hotly debated by students of cultural and media studies, by philosophers and by literary critics.

Benjamin wrote brilliant commentaries on major figures of literary modernism including Baudelaire, Proust, Kafka, Brecht and the Surrealists. He wrote as a modernist and his preoccupation with questions of language and with literary and artistic form extended to his experimental ways of conceiving and presenting his own writings.
Benjamin's writing is fragmentary, highly idiosyncratic, some of it even obscure. His major work, **The Paris Arcades**, was left incomplete. He aimed to restore a 'heightened graphicness' to the understanding of history, drawing on the emblem books of the 17th century and on the example of photomontage, as pioneered in his own day.

Benjamin For Beginners ™ uses the possibilities offered by the format of the documentary comic book to further extend Benjamin's experiments. It is a book which allows us to visualise what is involved in Benjamin's most subtle and unfinished meditations, as well as in his most revolutionary and radical gestures.

ASTENADA FOR BEGINNERS ™
Martin Broussalis
Illustrated by Martin Arvallo
ISBN 0-86316-068-9
(U.K. £7.99)

december 1998

In the summer of 1960, Carlos Castaneda was a student of Latin-American Anthropology, based in California. Academic logical reasoning had become ingrained in him. He was carrying out research into hallucinogenic plants in the Mexican desert. He met with the sorcerer Don Juan Matus, whose knowledge of the Toltec tradition went back thousands of years. Don Juan initiated Castaneda through a lengthy apprenticeship, which was by no means easy. During that time he saw all his convictions falling away, transforming himself despite himself, by entering into the magical universe pointed out to him by the sorcerer. Following the teachings passed on to him by Don Juan, Castaneda wrote a string of books describing his initiation, the other worlds discovered through new ways of seeing, and his experiences with the group of apprentices and sorcerers.

In **Castaneda For Beginners™**, the Argentinean novelist Martin Broussalis follows the path of Castaneda through these new dimensions of knowledge, arriving at the present time and Castaneda's position of shaman, transmitting under the name of Tensegrity his range of energising exercises.

accept **no** substitute!

> Great ideas and great thinkers can be thrilling. They can also be intimidating

That's where **Writers and Readers For Beginners**™ books come in. **Writers and Readers** brought you the <u>very</u> <u>first</u> **For Beginners**™ book over twenty years ago. Since then, amidst a growing number of imitators, we've published some 80 titles (ranging from Architecture to Zen and Einstein to Elvis) in the internationally acclaimed **For Beginners**™ series. Every book in the series serves one purpose: to UNintimidate and UNcomplicate the works of the great thinkers. Knowledge is too important to be confined to the experts.

And Knowledge as you will discover in our **Documentary Comic Books,** is fun! Each book is painstakingly researched, humorously written and illustrated in whatever style best suits the subject at hand. That's where **Writers and Readers, For Beginners**™ books began! Remember if it doesn't say...

Writers and Readers

...it's not an original For Beginners book.